EXAMINING WHAT A NUCLEAR IRAN DEAL MEANS FOR GLOBAL SECURITY

HEARING

BEFORE THE

SUBCOMMITTEE ON
THE MIDDLE EAST AND NORTH AFRICA

OF THE

COMMITTEE ON FOREIGN AFFAIRS
HOUSE OF REPRESENTATIVES

ONE HUNDRED THIRTEENTH CONGRESS

SECOND SESSION

NOVEMBER 20, 2014

Serial No. 113–224

Printed for the use of the Committee on Foreign Affairs

Available via the World Wide Web: http://www.foreignaffairs.house.gov/ or
http://www.gpo.gov/fdsys/

U.S. GOVERNMENT PRINTING OFFICE

91–459PDF   WASHINGTON : 2014

For sale by the Superintendent of Documents, U.S. Government Printing Office
Internet: bookstore.gpo.gov   Phone: toll free (866) 512–1800; DC area (202) 512–1800
Fax: (202) 512–2104   Mail: Stop IDCC, Washington, DC 20402–0001

COMMITTEE ON FOREIGN AFFAIRS

EDWARD R. ROYCE, California, *Chairman*

CHRISTOPHER H. SMITH, New Jersey
ILEANA ROS-LEHTINEN, Florida
DANA ROHRABACHER, California
STEVE CHABOT, Ohio
JOE WILSON, South Carolina
MICHAEL T. McCAUL, Texas
TED POE, Texas
MATT SALMON, Arizona
TOM MARINO, Pennsylvania
JEFF DUNCAN, South Carolina
ADAM KINZINGER, Illinois
MO BROOKS, Alabama
TOM COTTON, Arkansas
PAUL COOK, California
GEORGE HOLDING, North Carolina
RANDY K. WEBER SR., Texas
SCOTT PERRY, Pennsylvania
STEVE STOCKMAN, Texas
RON DeSANTIS, Florida
DOUG COLLINS, Georgia
MARK MEADOWS, North Carolina
TED S. YOHO, Florida
SEAN DUFFY, Wisconsin
CURT CLAWSON, Florida

ELIOT L. ENGEL, New York
ENI F.H. FALEOMAVAEGA, American Samoa
BRAD SHERMAN, California
GREGORY W. MEEKS, New York
ALBIO SIRES, New Jersey
GERALD E. CONNOLLY, Virginia
THEODORE E. DEUTCH, Florida
BRIAN HIGGINS, New York
KAREN BASS, California
WILLIAM KEATING, Massachusetts
DAVID CICILLINE, Rhode Island
ALAN GRAYSON, Florida
JUAN VARGAS, California
BRADLEY S. SCHNEIDER, Illinois
JOSEPH P. KENNEDY III, Massachusetts
AMI BERA, California
ALAN S. LOWENTHAL, California
GRACE MENG, New York
LOIS FRANKEL, Florida
TULSI GABBARD, Hawaii
JOAQUIN CASTRO, Texas

AMY PORTER, *Chief of Staff*   THOMAS SHEEHY, *Staff Director*
JASON STEINBAUM, *Democratic Staff Director*

SUBCOMMITTEE ON THE MIDDLE EAST AND NORTH AFRICA

ILEANA ROS-LEHTINEN, Florida, *Chairman*

STEVE CHABOT, Ohio
JOE WILSON, South Carolina
ADAM KINZINGER, Illinois
TOM COTTON, Arkansas
RANDY K. WEBER SR., Texas
RON DeSANTIS, Florida
DOUG COLLINS, Georgia
MARK MEADOWS, North Carolina
TED S. YOHO, Florida
SEAN DUFFY, Wisconsin
CURT CLAWSON, Florida

THEODORE E. DEUTCH, Florida
GERALD E. CONNOLLY, Virginia
BRIAN HIGGINS, New York
DAVID CICILLINE, Rhode Island
ALAN GRAYSON, Florida
JUAN VARGAS, California
BRADLEY S. SCHNEIDER, Illinois
JOSEPH P. KENNEDY III, Massachusetts
GRACE MENG, New York
LOIS FRANKEL, Florida

CONTENTS

Page

WITNESSES

LETTERS, STATEMENTS, ETC., SUBMITTED FOR THE HEARING

APPENDIX

EXAMINING WHAT A NUCLEAR IRAN DEAL MEANS FOR GLOBAL SECURITY

THURSDAY, NOVEMBER 20, 2014

House of Representatives,
Subcommittee on the Middle East and North Africa,
Committee on Foreign Affairs,
Washington, DC.

The subcommittee met, pursuant to notice, at 2 o'clock p.m., in room 2172, Rayburn House Office Building, Hon. Ileana Ros-Lehtinen (chairman of the subcommittee) presiding.

Ms. Ros-Lehtinen. This subcommittee will come to order.

After recognizing myself and Ranking Member Deutch for 5 minutes each for our opening statements, I will recognize other members seeking recognition.

We will then hear from our witnesses, and, without objection, the witnesses prepared statements will be made a part of the record. Members may have 5 days in which to insert statements and questions for the record, subject to the length limitation in the rules.

The Chair now recognizes herself for 5 minutes.

We are now just a few days away from the Iran nuclear deadline, and the P5+1 appear poised to accept a weak deal with a regime that cannot be trusted.

Despite approximately $14 billion in direct sanctions relief, as well as incalculable indirect benefits to the Iranian economy and the nuclear program, Iran has repeatedly stated that it will never stop enriching uranium or take one step back in its research and development.

Despite a 4-month extension of talks and allowing Iran access to an additional $700 million of its blocked currency each month, Iran's Supreme Leader 2 weeks ago called for the destruction of our greatest ally in the Middle East, the Democratic Jewish State of Israel.

Iran recently claimed its ballistic missiles are capable of razing Israeli cities and American military bases in the region to the ground. Iran has called for a Palestinian incitement against Israel, the result of which can be seen in the tragic murders 2 days ago of five Israelis, three of whom were U.S. Citizens in Jerusalem synagogue as they were praying.

From the onset, Iran has not complied with the terms outlined by the P5+1, exporting more oil than allowed, continuing production at the Arak heavy water reactor, denying access to key facilities, and dragging its feet every step of the way. The International Atomic Energy Agency has confirmed that Iran isn't even cooperating with its past commitments, such as completely disclosing its past work on nuclear weaponization.

Rouhani, who bragged in the past about deceiving the administration, as its chief negotiator, is known for using stall tactics while continuing to advance Iran's nuclear weapons program behind the scenes. And our leadership in the White House falls for it.

The administration turns a blind eye to Iran's support of terrorism, its constant threats against the United States and our allies, and its failure to cooperate even during this negotiation period. It ignores every lesson we thought we learned when North Korea delayed its way into a nuclear weapon. President Obama even sends secret letters to the Supreme Leader, naively hoping to appeal to the rational side of a man who has proven himself to be anything but.

The Iranians have made clear that no matter what a final deal contains, they will not stop enrichment and will not allow access to sites like Parchin and who knows how many other covert sites.

As General Hayden has stated, because of the covert nature of Iran's activities, American intelligence alone will not be able to verify the agreement. And, if he would still be advising the President, he would tell him that this deal could not be adequately verified.

Iran must be completely transparent about its current and past programs, including its weaponization programs and accept snap inspections anywhere, any time. But experience and a track record tells us that Iran will not do so. It is impossible to verify Iran's nuclear program because, as a Defense Science Board report has said, ''The capability to detect Iran's undeclared or covert nuclear sites is either inadequate or does not exist.''

Finally, the administration has misunderstood the point of sanctions, sanctions that Congress worked hard to build from the very beginning. The sanctions regime that Congress put into place was designed to work together. The sanctions are interconnected to target, not just the nuclear program, but Iran's ballistic weapons program and human rights abuses as well.

The P5+1 has allowed Iran's economy to grow, its currency to strengthen, and has provided a dangerous amount of concessions and sanctions relief to the regime based only on its nuclear program. And they have given Iran the time and money it needs to be more resilient and even better able to weather sanctions in the future. The effect of sanctions takes time and it cannot be easily re-implemented or once lifted or once suspended.

Yet all indications are that President Obama, if a final deal is reached, would seek to lift sanctions or use waiver authority provided within the sanctions law. These waivers, however, are national security waivers. It is not in the national security interest of the United States to provide Iran additional access to cash with which it can proliferate and expand other ilicit activities, specifically, its support for global terror.

Just last week, the President reissued a continuation of the national emergency with respect to Iran, a status which has been in place since the Iran hostage crisis in 1979. It strains the imagination to see how the President can, on one hand, declare Iran as a national emergency, yet on the other waive sanctions and say, Iran is not a national security threat. Congress needs to reclaim its sanction authority from this administration, do everything it can to prevent this weak deal from happening.

So let me be clear, no matter what the P5+1 does, Congress should not allow a deal that threatens our national security interest to stand, and we intend on repairing the damage that has been done as soon as possible. We must reinstate and expand sanctions, and we must not allow Iran to get a nuclear bomb.

Either the P5+1 secures the deal that includes the complete cessation of Iran's enrichment and the full dismantling of its nuclear infrastructure or it must walk away from these doomed talks altogether.

And with that, I am pleased to yield to my good friend from Florida, the ranking member, Congressman Ted Deutch.

Mr. DEUTCH. Thank you, Madam Chairman.

Thanks for holding this extremely timely hearing as we are just 4 days away from the November 24th deadline to reach a deal to prevent Iran from acquiring a nuclear weapon.

Madam Chairman, often we are told these hearings that—often when we are told that, in these hearings, we have important points to make, 5 minutes is not enough to lay out the complex issues that we are tackling in the Middle East. But today it really comes down to one simple question. Will we prevent Iran from acquiring nuclear weapons capabilities?

I don't think any of us are under the illusion that a satisfactory and comprehensive deal will be reached on Monday. But let me be clear, any deal must cut off all of Iran's pathways to a nuclear weapon; and this specifically includes the Arak reactor. A deal must dismantle Iran's centrifuge program to prevent Iran from becoming a threshold nuclear state, create robust verification and monitoring mechanisms to prevent undetectable breakout, force Iran to come clean on its past nuclear activities, including impossible military dimensions and cover a long enough duration that the regime won't simply wait it out.

In the absence of a deal on Monday, we could be left with alternative outcomes. Either an extension of talks under the current terms or framework agreement with details to be addressed in the future negotiations or final recognition that the clerics running around never intended to make a deal at all. Any suggestion that talks should be extended must include verifiable mechanisms to prevent Iran from covertly advancing its nuclear program.

Madam Chairman, I can't stress enough to our negotiators in Vienna and our P5+1 partners how seriously we take the implementation of a strict verification and monitoring process. This regime has unfortunately proven itself untrustworthy time and time again. We have uncovered covert nuclear facilities. We have discovered military dimensions to its nuclear program, the development and testing of ballistic missiles, the arms shipped to terrorist groups, all in direct violation of United Nations Security Council resolutions.

If an extension is suggested, it must be for a clearly defined and limited time. Iran cannot be allowed to negotiate in perpetuity, dragging things out while continuing to receive sanctions relief in exchange for incremental baby steps. The current status quo will not be the accepted new normal. Now is the time for Iran to take significant steps to show the world, once and for all, whether or not it is serious.

And if an extension is proposed, Congress should make clear to Iran that sanctions will be ratcheted up dramatically at the expiration of an extension period. This will finally make Iran understand the ramifications of failing to yield on its pursuit of a nuclear weapon.

And while the world has been focused for the past year on nuclear negotiations, this regime has continued to engage in the most egregious human rights abuses against its own people, something that we hear too little about. Make no mistake, deal or no deal, we will not continue—we will not overlook Iran's abysmal human rights record.

Yesterday, United Nations issued a strong rebuke to the regime on human rights, adopting a resolution criticizing Iran—and I quote—''alarming high frequency and increase in the death penalty, widespread restrictions on basic freedoms and worsening discrimination and persecution of women and minorities.''

This regime, during the Rouhani presidency, has executed over 850 people in the past 15 months. This includes 12 executions in one prison over 11 days in October. Religious minorities, women, and the LGBT community continue to be persecuted. Access to free press and the internet is blocked. Communications are monitored and people are detained for expressing dissent toward regime policies.

Iran has not fulfilled its promises of assistance in our efforts as well to find my constituent, Robert Levinson, who has now been missing and separated from his wife, children, and grandchildren for 2,813 days. It has not released the other Americans imprisoned or Washington Post journalist, Jason Rezaian, who has been held without charges for over 120 days.

This regime may no longer have the bombastic spokesman, Ahmadinejad, to incite anti-Semitism and spew vitriol. But that hasn't stopped the Supreme Leader from issuing just recently a nine-point plan on why and how Israel should be annihilated. It hasn't stopped the regime's unabated support for the murderous Assad regime, or it relentless support for Hezbollah's terrorism around the world. It hasn't stopped its meddling in Iraq, and Yemen, and Bahrain, and other Gulf countries.

Look, I want to see a diplomatic solution to the nuclear crisis. The best resolution would be to reach a comprehensive deal that addresses all of the points that I laid out earlier. But even if a nuclear deal is reached, Iran must know that its behavior will not be accepted by responsible Nations. We will speak out against the regime's barbaric treatment of its own people. We will continue to enforce sanctions on those who perpetuate these abuses. And we will continue to go after the regime's financial and military support of terrorist organizations.

I know we are all anxiously awaiting Monday's deadline, and I would just like to repeat what we have heard from the administration since day one, ''No deal is better than a bad deal.'' A bad deal will gravely threaten the safety and security of the United States, of our allies in the region, especially Israel.

And, Madam Chairman, let me be clear about one last thing, those of us who may question the merits of an inadequate deal are not on a march and do not advocate a march to war. We simply do not want to see an agreement that allows Iran to acquire a nuclear weapon right under our noses.

Again, I thank our witnesses for appearing today. You each bring unique expertise and insight into Iran's domestic and foreign policy, and I look forward to a productive discussion.

I yield back.

Ms. ROS-LEHTINEN. Thank you very much, Mr. Deutch.

And now I will recognize other members for their opening statements.

Mr. Wilson of South Carolina.

Mr. WILSON. Thank you, Madam Chairman.

And I would like to join in with Congressman Deutch to reiterate that this is an untrustworthy regime. It is untrustworthy to its citizens, indeed the violations of human rights, the subjugation of the women of Iran.

We know this is the great culture of Persia. More should be expected of such an extraordinary country, but the people are being subjugated. And, then, at the same time, we have an American administration that, I think, is being extraordinarily naive.

Our country, we should remember the inhumanity of the hostage crisis, the taking of our Embassy in 1979, violating every norms of civilized law, international law. Additionally, I will never forget that it was Iran that directed the bombing of the Marine barracks at Beirut, hundreds of Americans were killed. It was the largest explosion since Nagasaki. And then the IEDs provided to terrorists to kill American personnel, Iraq, Afghanistan. Having two sons serve in Iraq, another in Afghanistan, it was quite personal to me.

We should remember that their signs carried, in English for our benefit, ''Death to America. Death to Israel.'' And that is the way the negotiations should be conducted as people not trustworthy.

Thank you.

Ms. ROS-LEHTINEN. Thank you very much, Mr. Wilson.

Mr. Higgins of New York.

Mr. HIGGINS. Thank you, Madam Chair, for holding this important hearing.

The nuclear—a nuclear Iran would have severe repercussions for America's security and that of our allies, further destabilizing an already volatile region and emboldening a already dangerous regime.

Preventing Iran from obtaining a nuclear weapon is a major strategic imperative of the United States and must be continued. As the deadline for concluding a nuclear deal approaches, it is useful to provide some context on the evolution of Iran's nuclear program. In the past, Iran cynically used the negotiations process with the EU Nations in order to continue enrichment activities and protect itself from United States intervention. Now, Iran has built out its capacity to 19,000 centrifuges.

Stiff sanctions are what brought Iran to the table, and they must continue to be our leverage point. I fear that by continuing to provide sanctions relief in exchange for vague commitments by the

Iranians, we are helping to rehabilitate an Iranian economy and eroding a robust and effective sanctions policy.

I look forward to the testimony of our witnesses.

Thank you. I yield back.

Ms. ROS-LEHTINEN. Thank you, sir.

Dr. Yoho.

Dr. YOHO. I have no opening statement, Madam Chair.

Ms. ROS-LEHTINEN. Mr. DeSantis.

Mr. DESANTIS. Thank you, Madam Chairwoman, for holding this important hearing and your diligence on this subject.

You know, between the time we left before the election and re-convene, there were two troubling reports. One was the report of the President writing a letter to the Ayatollah about potential common interests that we may have with Iran to fight ISIS, and then the other report that was troubling was that the Iran deal was most likely to be constructed in a way to avoid scrutiny by Congress.

And so I looked at that and said, they want Iran to be a constructive force in Iraq and what type of consideration are they going to provide in these nuclear negotiations, because I don't think we are likely to be successful anyways. And I really fear that we could be running into a catastrophic policy outcome, and I think it is very incumbent on the Congress to insert ourselves in this.

We should not allow a bad deal to go without us having to vote and, if it is a bad deal, then, we need to be strong and impose sanctions. There would have been sanctions to pass the Senate, except for one man, Harry Reid, would not let that come for a vote. In January, there is a new sheriff in town.

And I yield back.

Ms. ROS-LEHTINEN. Thank you, Mr. DeSantis.

Mr. Vargas of California.

Mr. VARGAS. Thank you very much, Madam Chair.

And witnesses for being here today.

I have always believed that it has been naive to negotiate with Iran over their nuclear program. I think the Iranians, their negotiating policy, really is to stall and they have stalled. And they have extended, and they have extended. I think they are going to continue to do that.

I thought the appropriate approach was to pass more comprehensive sanctions. I did that here, and I thought that they had to really pick, then, between they want an economy that functioned, a society, or did they want their nuclear program. They couldn't have both. Unfortunately, we are down this path, and it looks like they want to extend and stall once again.

I hope that we will get back to the sanctions. I hope that we pass stronger sanctions, and I think that that is the way to go. They have to make a decision. Do you want this nuclear program, or do you want a functioning society?

I thank you again, Madam Chair, for holding this hearing.

Ms. ROS-LEHTINEN. Thank you, sir.

Ms. Frankel of Florida.

Ms. FRANKEL. Thank you, Madam Chair.

I think we are all mindful that one of the ramifications of Iran obtaining nuclear weapons is the potential of proliferation in the region. And so, as you testify today, I would be interested in hearing what other countries you think might seek to obtain nuclear weapons and how would that relate to what is going on with ISIL?

Ms. ROS-LEHTINEN. Very good question.

Thank you.

Ms. FRANKEL. I yield the rest of my time.

Ms. ROS-LEHTINEN. Mr. Cicilline of Rhode Island.

Mr. CICILLINE. Thank you, Madam Chairman, and Ranking Member Deutch for holding today's hearing on this issue that is really vital to the U.S. national security interests.

The continuing threat that Iran poses to international stability is of paramount concern to the United States and to our national security interest. I certainly appreciate the efforts made by the administration and the P5+1 in negotiations with Iran pursuant to the terms of the joint plan of action, but serious questions remain regarding Iran's interest in reaching a final deal and Iran's intention of arming the terms of any agreement, even if one were reached.

While reports suggests that some small progress has been made in the negotiations, we must remain vigilant to ensure that any comprehensive deal truly protects the national security interests of the United States and our allies around the world. We will need to ensure that Iran complies with international law and any restrictions and requirements agreed to in a final deal are verifiable and, also, guarantee that Iran is unable to develop a nuclear weapons capability, period.

Finally, I want to note that it is crucial that Congress and the administration continue to work together, not separately to best achieve the foreign policy priorities of the United States, an agreement that once and for all prevents a nuclear Iran.

I thank you, and I yield back.

Ms. ROS-LEHTINEN. Thank you, sir.

Mr. Connolly of Virginia.

Mr. CONNOLLY. Thank you, Madam Chairman.

Madam Chairman, let's stipulate, we don't like Iran. Let's also stipulate we don't want a nuclear Iran. They are two different things to conflate the need for domestic reform in Iran to the point where it is pluralistic, democratic, inclusive, and respects all human rights, otherwise, we are never going to sit down with them and negotiate a nuclear deal, is a very perilous proposition. We don't live in an ideal world.

The interim agreement, according to the International Atomic Energy Agency, has produced pursuant to the agreement. There are no new centrifuges. Construction has been halted in a heavy water facility reactor at Arak. Five percent uranium 235 stockpiles remain at pre-JPOA levels, and 20 percent uranium 235 stockpiles have been eliminated. It ain't perfect. We would like to finalize a final agreement. But if we make perfect be the enemy of the good, we are condemning the world to a confrontation over Iran. And I think most Americans want to avoid that if that is possible.

Thank you, Madam Chairman.

Ms. ROS-LEHTINEN. Thank you, sir.

Mr. Schneider of Illinois.

Mr. SCHNEIDER. Thank you, Madam Chairwoman, and thank you for calling this hearing. Thank you for your profound remarks.

Also, the ranking member, Mr. Deutch, I want to associate myself with those remarks as well.

There is no newspaper big enough to cover all of the issues happening around the world today. But every day, not just today, every day the number one story at the top of the fold has to be preventing a nuclear Iran.

If there is going to be a deal, it must only be a good deal. And a good deal will only be such if it blocks all of Iran's pathways to a nuclear weapon and not temporarily, but permanently across generations. It has to be a deal that blocks their programs for enrichment, weaponization, and delivery systems. But it must also deal with Iran's support of international terrorism and Iran's threats to the region as well as its human rights violations. We must have a deal that blocks that and protects, not just the region, but the entire world.

I look forward to hearing from all of our witnesses to hear what you have to say how we might best get to the that or what happens if we don't.

Thank you.

Ms. ROS-LEHTINEN. Thank you, sir.

And now I will turn to Mr. Cotton of Arkansas.

Mr. COTTON. Thank you.

In the interest of time, I will speak very briefly and just say that I am doubtful that any deal could be reached with this Iranian regime that would stop this Iranian regime from pursuing nuclear weapons, and I hope that the President will take the right action to keep America and our allies safe in the region.

And I look forward to hearing what the witnesses have to say on these matters.

Ms. ROS-LEHTINEN. Thank you, sir.

Mr. Kennedy of Massachusetts.

Mr. KENNEDY. Madam Chair, than you very much.

To the ranking member, thank you both for hosting an important hearing.

To the witnesses, thank you for, once again, appearing before this committee and thank you for your service to our country as well.

There are a number of issues obviously before this Congress and before the next one. Very few have the potential of a generational impact like an Iranian nuclear weapon and the cascading effects throughout the region. I would ask to—I would like—I want to get to your testimony, your comments.

I would like to hear from the witnesses at some point, if you can speculate a little bit, assuming that a deal is not reached on the 24th, what happens then, particularly with regards to, I would say three points in building off my colleague, Ms. Frankel, with regards to Russia and our relationship with Russia, with regards to Iraq, and with regards to ISIL and Syria?

Thank you very much.

Ms. ROS-LEHTINEN. Thank you, sir.

And now I will introduce our witnesses.

First, we are all very pleased to welcome General Michael Hayden, who has had a very impressive and distinguished career. Over his 40-year career, he rose through the ranks to become a Four-Star General, the Director of the National Security Agency, the first Principal Deputy Director of National Intelligence and the Director of the Central Intelligence Agency. General Hayden is now a principal with the Chertoff Group, and we welcome him here today and we thank him for his service. Thank you very much, General.

Next, we welcome back to our committee Mr. Mark Dubowitz, executive director of the Foundation for Defense of Democracies, where he leads projects on Iran, sanctions, proliferation, as the head of FDD's center on sanctions and ilicit finance. Mr. Dubowitz is the author of 15 studies on economic sanctions against Iran, and he is also co-chair of the project on U.S.-Middle East nonproliferation strategy. Welcome, Mark.

And, finally, we also welcome back Mr. Karim Sadjadpour, a senior associate at the Carnegie Endowment for International Peace. Prior to this, Mr. Sadjadpour was the chief Iran analyst at the International Crisis Group and he is a board member of the Banu Foundation, an organization dedicated to empowering women worldwide.

We are very pleased with the high quality of our witnesses today; your prepared remarks will be made a part of the record. Please feel free to synthesize them for us.

General Hayden, we will begin with you, sir.

STATEMENT OF GENERAL MICHAEL HAYDEN, USAF, RETIRED, PRINCIPAL, THE CHERTOFF GROUP (FORMER DIRECTOR OF THE CENTRAL INTELLIGENCE AGENCY)

General HAYDEN. Thank you, ma'am, and thanks for the opportunity to testify today.

In the nearly 6 years since I have left government, people have asked me, ''What keeps you awake at night?'' Iran has always been in my list. In fact, let me add that Iran was the problem with which I was least satisfied when I left government in February 2009. We certainly did not hand our successors a pretty package here.

And so I said to myself, with the questions Mr. Schneider and Mr. Kennedy brought up, it is the problem I think that has most consistently continued to worsen in the intervening 5½ years.

Now, we are involved in nuclear negotiations with the Islamic republic and, no doubt, as you have pointed out, that is the product of the tough sanctions that two administrations have levied against Tehran. Now, the real question before us is, can we come out of these negotiations with a nuclear agreement that will give us confidence that we will have the time, the certainty, and the will to prevent Iran from becoming a nuclear weapon state at any time in the future?

Now, I come at this as a professional intelligence officer, so I will keep my remarks pretty much in that lane.

First point I would like to make is Iran is a tough intelligence target. During my time as Director of CIA, Iran was the second most discussed topic in the Oval Office. The only one more discussed was terrorism. And, frankly, there wasn't a number three. I mean, we talked about a lot of other things, but we didn't aggregate around it like we did terrorism and Iran.

President Bush used to ask me two kinds of questions. One basket was, ''What does the program look like? How much low-enrich uranium, how many centrifuges?'' The other basket of questions was simply, ''How do these guys make decisions? How do I influence their processes going forward?''

I always wanted the nuclear questions because Iran is an incredibly, incredibly opaque society. So we should be under no illusions that we can precisely define the motivations or the future plans of the various power centers that vie for control in Tehran today. So that gives me little confidence about any plan of action predicated on helping the moderates in Tehran.

Second, our knowledge of the Iranian nuclear program is incomplete. That is why I believe an important element of any agreement has to be far more transparent than we have today about the past history of Iranian nuclear efforts. It is particularly disheartening, as you said, Madam Chairman, when the IAEA is denied access to facilities and information that they think they need to judge Iranian compliance.

Look, the objective of these talks is to put distance between where the Iranians are parked and where they have to be to have a weapon. It is near impossible for us to judge whether the distance is adequate without a full accounting of the work they have done to date in secrecy.

Third, even with incomplete knowledge on the program, it is my belief that, at a minimum, Iran is keeping its options open, working very hard to keep its options open for a nuclear weapon. There is no other logical explanation for their investment in time, energy, commerce, and prestige that they have been willing to make.

Now, I say that fully aware that I was in government when we produced a national intelligence estimate in 2007 that said that Iran had stopped a part of its nuclear weapons program. And that judgment was not based on the absence of evidence. It was indeed based on evidence of absence. They had stopped some work, but that was far more tactical than strategic. Some of that work has resumed in other important aspects, like creating fissile material and ballistic missile technology. That continued to pace.

A fourth point. Iran is already close to a weapon—too close to a weapon. The point of the negotiations, from our point of view, has to be to roll the program back, not freeze it in place. That means that certain activities, stocks, facilities have to be dismantled. From all accounts, the Iranians have not been very forthcoming on that important subject; and so I would be very cautious about creative solutions that have been put forward in place of the actual dismantlement of facilities and equipment and stockpiles.

Ms. Frankel, an Iran that is parked too close to a nuclear weapon will pretty much have the same destabilizing effect on the region as an Iran that has just tested a nuclear weapon. The Sunni neighbors will draw their conclusions, and they will act accordingly, and I know that this committee understands how harmful that would be for the entire region.

A fifth and final point has to do with verification. I had to deal with this question at the end of the Bush administration when we were negotiating with the North Koreans. At that time, in NSC meetings, I pressed for an invasive verification regime as a necessity for any agreement because I was unwilling to guarantee that American intelligence could sufficiently verify the agreement on its own.

So let me repeat that position for the question before us today. Absent an invasive inspection regime, with freedom to visit even suspect sites on short notice, American intelligence cannot provide adequate warning of Iranian nuclear developments.

I know there are many other aspects of the issue that the committee will want to explore, and I look forward to that discussion, ma'am.

Ms. Ros-Lehtinen. Thank you so much. That was very clear.

[The prepared statement of General Hayden follows:]

Testimony before the House Committee on Foreign Affairs

Michael V. Hayden
Gen., USAF, retired
Former Director CIA and NSA

Examining what a Nuclear Iran Deal Means for Global Security

20 November 2014

Madame Chairman, thank you for the opportunity to testify before the committee today. In the nearly 6 years since I have left government, I have continued in my public speeches to consistently include Iran and its nuclear program among the five things that "keep me awake at night".

In fact, let me add that Iran was the problem with which I was least satisfied when I left government service in February, 2009. And it is the problem that has most consistently continued to worsen since that date.

We are now involved in nuclear negotiations with the Islamic Republic, no doubt the product of the tough sanctions created by the last two administrations. The real question, I believe, that is before us is what kind of nuclear agreement makes the situation better than it is today.

In fact, the bar is even higher. What kind of nuclear agreement will give us confidence that we will have the time, the certainty, and the will to prevent Iran becoming a nuclear weapons state at any time in the future?

I, of course, come at this problem from my professional perspective as an intelligence officer. And I will confine my comments to that aspect in this opening statement. Of course, I will welcome questions on broader topics from committee members later.

First, everyone must understand that Iran is a difficult intelligence target. During my time as director of CIA Iran was the second most discussed topic in the Oval Office, coming in behind only terrorism. President Bush used to ask me two kinds of questions about Iran. The first type would be obvious: what is the status of the Iranian nuclear program? The second type was simply to explain to him the decision-making processes inside the Islamic Republic. I always preferred the first type of question. The Iranian decision-making process is incredibly opaque and we should be under no illusions that we can precisely define the motivations or the future plans of the various power centers that vie for control in Teheran today. That gives me little confidence about any plans of action that are predicated on "helping the moderates" in that capital.

Second, our knowledge of the Iranian nuclear program is incomplete. That is why I believe that an important element of any agreement must be far more transparency than we have today about the past history of Iranian nuclear efforts. It is particularly disheartening when the IAEA is denied access to information or to installations they believe they need to see in order to gauge Iran's compliance with past agreements.

If the objective of these talks is to put distance between where the Iranians are and where they have to be to have a weapon, then we need a full accounting of the work they have done to date. Current American intelligence paints a picture inconsistent with Iranian claims, but no one on our side would say we yet have a complete picture of their work to date.

Third, even with incomplete knowledge, it is my assessment that at a minimum Iran is working very hard to keep its nuclear weapons option available. There is no other logical explanation for the investment in time, energy, commerce and national prestige that Iran has been willing to make.

I say this fully aware of the 2007 National Intelligence Estimate that judged that Iran had stopped at least a part of its program to develop a nuclear weapon. That assessment, I must add, was based upon evidence of absence, not absence of evidence. In other words, we did have good data that certain aspects of the program had been stopped. I judge that was far more a tactical than a strategic decision, however. And other aspects of the program continued forward with great energy. Here of course I am talking about Iranian work on creating fissile material and Iranian work in developing its ballistic missile force.

A fourth point. Iran is already too close to a nuclear weapon. The point of the negotiations from our point of view must be to roll back the Iranian program, not freeze it in place. That means that certain activities, certain stocks, and certain facilities must be dismantled. From all accounts, the Iranians have not yet been willing to be very forthcoming on this very important aspect. I would be very cautious about "creative solutions" that have been put forward in place of actual dismantlement of facilities and equipment and stockpiles.

An Iran that is parked too close to nuclear weapon's breakout will have a destabilizing effect on the region much like an Iran that has just tested a nuclear weapon. The Sunni neighbors will draw their conclusions and they will act accordingly. And, I believe, the committee understands how harmful that would be for the region and for us.

A fifth point that I believe should be made deals with verification. I had to deal with this question near the end of the Bush administration when we were negotiating with the North Koreans. At that time I pressed for invasive verification as a necessity for any agreement since I was unwilling to guarantee that American intelligence could sufficiently verify the agreement on its own. Let me repeat that position for the question before us today. Absent an invasive inspection regime, with freedom to visit all sites on short notice, American intelligence cannot provide adequate warning of Iranian nuclear developments.

I know that there are many other aspects of this issue that the committee will want to explore. I look forward to that important discussion.

———————

Ms. ROS-LEHTINEN. Mr. Dubowitz.

STATEMENT OF MR. MARK DUBOWITZ, EXECUTIVE DIRECTOR, FOUNDATION FOR DEFENSE OF DEMOCRACIES

Mr. DUBOWITZ. Chairman Ros-Lehtinen, Ranking Member Deutch, members of the subcommittee, on behalf of FDD, thank you for inviting me again to testify.

I am honored and certainly humbled to be testifying with General Hayden and with Karim Sadjadpour, whose work and service to our country I greatly admire.

As many of you have said, Iran is at this negotiation table because of you, because of the sanctions that you have passed. Now, Congress has attempted to do other things. You have attempted to establish clear parameters for what constitutes an acceptable nuclear deal. You have attempted to put in place sanctions and waiting to increase American leverage. You have attempted to set a strict timeline for the conclusion of a deal, and you have attempted to demand that a final deal should be put to a vote in Congress.

The administration has blocked all of these efforts. Congress should continue pushing on all of these fronts, but it should also defend the very sanctions architecture that was so instrumental in creating. This is going to be essential to enforce any Iranian nuclear deal, to provide increased leverage to respond to Iranian noncompliance, and to deter and punish Iran's elicit activities. Because after detection, what? What leverage are we going to have left to force the Iranians back into compliance?

Now, a negotiated agreement is the preferred solution to peacefully resolve this nuclear crisis. Iran's record of nuclear deception, its sponsorship of terrorism, it egregious human rights abuses, all of this does not inspire confidence in Tehran's commitment to honor a final nuclear agreement.

Moreover, the administration may not be demanding the best deal it can get. Administration officials are on record actually, in the past 7, 8 months as committing to a deal that will ''dismantle'' ''a lot'' or ''significant portions'' of Iran's nuclear infrastructure. But the terms of a deal could fall far short of that. The more flawed the deal, the more important it will be for Congress to defend the sanctions architecture to maintain economic leverage.

Now, the administration has reportedly studied how it might suspend the ''vast majority of sanctions'' after a nuclear deal while bypassing you. In response, Congress needs to stand behind the July 2014 letter that was signed by 344 members of the House of Representatives. It affirmed ''that the concept of an exclusively defined nuclear-related sanction on Iran does not exist in U.S. law'' and that ''almost all sanctions related to Iran's nuclear program are also related to Tehran's advancing ballistic missile program, intensifying support for international terrorism and other unconventional weapons programs.''

Based on press reports, it appears that the administration and perhaps the EU and the U.N. Security Council are designing a phased program of sanctions relief, using suspensions and snapbacks where sanctions will be suspended and only reimposed in the event of Iranian noncompliance.

Now, the legalities of snapbacks are simple, but the politics and economics are very complicated. A premature suspension of U.S., UNSC, and EU sanctions an overreliance on snapbacks could seriously undermine the Iran sanctions regime and give Iran's nuclear program political legitimacy.

At the U.S.–EU UNSC, there would have to be agreement that there is sufficient evidence of Iranian noncompliance to warrant a decision to reinstate these sanctions. Significant disputes are inevitable about the seriousness of infractions, the appropriate level of response, and possible Iranian retaliation.

Furthermore—and this is a concern a number of members have expressed today—the administration may not respond effectively to evidence of Iranian noncompliance for fear that enforcement could prompt Iranian countermeasures. Now, this is particular disconcerting amidst reports of a growing U.S.-Iran detente and possible coordination to weaken ISIL.

The snapback is equally challenging to implement, given certain economic reality. Sanctions took years before international companies terminated their business ties with Tehran. Once loosened, it is going to very difficult to get those companies to leave again.

Iran also enjoyed substantial psychological benefits from inking a deal. That will translate into improved macroeconomic conditions as it already has under the JPOA. The administration seriously underestimated the value of sanctions relief under the JPOA. It did not account for the psychological impact on Iran's macroeconomic environment. As a result, Iran's economy has shown signs of stabilization, reflected in modest GDP growth, a stabilization of the currency, and a significant drop in inflation.

As Iran's economic recovery becomes less susceptible to snapback sanctions, economic pressure is going to be a less effective tool to respond to Iranian nuclear noncompliance. This will make it more likely that the U.S. will be forced to cheat—or forced to choose between either tolerating Iran's cheating or using military force to respond to violations. And that is unrealistic, given that this regime tends to cheat incrementally.

In my written testimony, I provide detailed recommendations in how Congress can defend its sanctions architecture, including how to limit ways the administration could act unilaterally.

In conclusion, Congress has a vital role to play to protect and enhance U.S. economic leverage, and this leverage is going to be essential to enforce a deal and pressure Tehran to end all of its ilicit activities. Thank you very much.

Ms. ROS-LEHTINEN. Thank you so much, Mr. Dubowitz.

[The prepared statement of Mr. Dubowitz follows:]

Congressional Testimony

Examining What a Nuclear Iran Deal Means for Global Security

Mark Dubowitz
Executive Director
Foundation for Defense of Democracies

**Hearing before the
House Committee on Foreign Affairs
Subcommittee on the Middle East and North Africa**

Washington, DC
November 20, 2014

DEFENSE OF DEMOCRACIES 1726 M Street NW • Suite 700 • Washington, DC 20036

Chairman Ros-Lehtinen, Ranking Member Deutch, members of the Subcommittee, on behalf of the Foundation for Defense of Democracies (FDD), thank you for inviting me to testify today. I am honored to be testifying with General Michael Hayden and Karim Sadjadpour, whose work I greatly admire.

Thank you for inviting me here today to discuss what an Iranian nuclear deal means for global security. I will focus on the role that Congress can play to enforce a comprehensive agreement, provide increased leverage to respond to Iranian nuclear non-compliance, and deter and punish the full range of Iran's illicit and dangerous activities. Congress can achieve these goals by defending the sanctions architecture that it was so instrumental in creating.

INTRODUCTION

A negotiated agreement is the preferred solution to peacefully prevent Iran from achieving a nuclear weapons capacity. Iran's record of nuclear deception, role as the leading state sponsor of terrorism, and egregious human rights abuses, however, does not inspire confidence in Tehran's commitment to honor a final nuclear agreement with the P5+1.

Moreover, America may not be demanding the best deal it can get. Administration officials are on record committing to a deal that will "dismantle" "a lot" or "significant" portions of Iran's nuclear infrastructure.

On November 24, 2013, Secretary of State John Kerry said:

> The [interim] deal is the beginning and first step. It leads us into the negotiation, so that we guarantee that while we are *negotiating for the dismantling*, while we are negotiating for the tougher positions, they will not grow their program and their capacity to threaten Israel (emphasis added).[1]

In December 2013, Secretary Kerry also explained that the purpose of sanctions is to help convince Iran to *dismantle* its nuclear program:

> I don't think that any of us thought we were just imposing these sanctions for the sake of imposing them. We did it because we knew that it would hopefully *help Iran dismantle its nuclear program*. That was the whole point of the [sanctions] regime (emphasis added).[2]

In December 2013, Under Secretary of State and lead U.S. negotiator in the P5+1 talks

---

[1] MaryAlice Parks, "Sec. John Kerry: 'No Daylight' Between Israel, U.S. on Goal for Iran Nuclear Program," *ABC News*, November 24, 2013. (http://abcnews.go.com/blogs/politics/2013/11/sec-john-kerry-no-daylight-between-israel-and-united-states/)
[2] John Kerry, "The P5+1's First Step Agreement With Iran on its Nuclear Program," *Testimony before the House Foreign Affairs Committee*, December 10, 2013.
(http://www.state.gov/secretary/remarks/2013/12/218578.htm)

Wendy Sherman said:

> This *includes a lot of dismantling of their infrastructure*, because, quite frankly, we're not quite sure what you need a 40-megawatt heavy water reactor, which is what Arak is, for any civilian peaceful purpose (emphasis added).[3]

In January 2014, White House Press Secretary Jay Carney said:

> Now, we have also been clear that as part of that comprehensive agreement, should it be reached, Iran will be required to agree to strict limits and constraints on all aspects of its nuclear program to include the *dismantlement of significant portions of its nuclear infrastructure* in order to prevent Iran from developing a nuclear weapon in the future (emphasis added).[4]

Based on press reporting and statements from administration officials, it now appears that the terms of a deal being negotiated in Vienna could fall short of the dismantlement of "significant" or "a lot" of Iran's nuclear program.[5] The reason: Iran has increased its negotiating leverage.

During the 2013 negotiations leading to the Joint Plan of Action (JPOA), the White House yielded to Supreme Leader Ali Khamenei's red lines against reducing enrichment capacity and foreclosing an industrial-size program. Iran thus continued uranium enrichment, building long-range ballistic missiles, and developing advanced centrifuges. Iran further refused to accept intrusive U.N. or other inspections, balked at dismantling the heavy-water reactor at Arak, and declined to discuss past weaponization research. It also pocketed a concession that any restrictions on its nuclear program would be of limited duration. When the restrictions expire, Iran will almost certainly have a large-scale, industrial-size civilian nuclear program, with an easier clandestine "sneak out" option, which could be used to rapidly produce nuclear weapons if the Iranian leadership elects to do so.

Tehran has treated the P5+1's concessions to its demands as permanent – effectively making further diplomatic advances contingent on greater Western "flexibility." P5+1 negotiators, by contrast, appear to be trying to find ways to accommodate Khamenei's red lines. Take, for instance, the recent American suggestion to disconnect the centrifuge

---

[3] "Lead Negotiator: U.S. Would Consider Limited Enrichment By Iran with Conditions," *PBS Newshour*, December 4, 2013. (http://www.pbs.org/newshour/bb/world-july-dec13-sherman_12-04/)
[4] The White House, "Press Briefing by Press Secretary Jay Carney," January 23, 2014. (http://m.whitehouse.gov/the-press-office/2014/01/23/press-briefing-press-secretary-jay-carney-1232014)
[5] Paul Richter & Ramin Mostaghim, "Report Says U.S. May OK More Centrifuges in Iran Nuclear Talks," *Los Angeles Times*, October 20, 2014; (http://www.latimes.com/world/middleeast/la-fg-iran-nuclear-20141021-story.html) & David Sanger, "U.S. Hopes Face-Saving Plan Offers a Path to a Nuclear Pact With Iran," *The New York Times*, September 19, 2014. (http://www.nytimes.com/2014/09/20/world/middleeast/us-hopes-face-saving-plan-offers-apath-to-a-nuclear-pact-with-iran-.html?_r=0)

piping at Iran's enrichment facilities instead of dismantling Iran's centrifuges entirely.[6] As it stands now, Iran would be able to easily resurrect its enrichment program in a few weeks, simply by reconnecting the piping.[7]

In another scenario, Iran could be required to disconnect all "excess" centrifuges and cascade piping used in the uranium-enrichment process at Iran's Natanz facility – and retire around 14,000 first-generation machines into storage under United Nations safeguards. Tehran might accept the proposal so long as advanced centrifuge development continues – and the 14,000 excess older centrifuges aren't disconnected unless they are swapped for fewer but more-advanced models, which can be reconnected much more quickly than the older ones. Any plan that would allow more advanced centrifuges to replace older models, even if the new models aren't enriching, could actually lead to Natanz becoming more efficient. This would dramatically reduce the amount of time Iran would need to enrich to weapons-grade uranium.

Iran's current sites, with their tested infrastructure, can also be used to perfect ever-more advanced centrifuges. This would make it far easier for Iran to build small, very-difficult-to-detect clandestine facilities that could enable Iran to "sneak out" or to reduce the time necessary to "break-out" at known, U.N. monitored installations.

It is also increasingly clear that a final agreement will fail to address Iran's ballistic missile program, despite the requirements of U.S. legislation and U.N. Security Council resolutions.[8] The P5+1 is apparently narrowly defining the ability to affix a warhead to a ballistic missile, as evidenced by Under Secretary of State Wendy Sherman, who stated in congressional testimony, "We must address long-range ballistic missiles capable of carrying nuclear warheads. So, it's not about ballistic missiles per se. It's about when a missile is combined with a nuclear warhead."[9] The exclusion of ballistic missiles themselves from the negotiations also raises verification and monitoring concerns. As the January 2014 report of the Defense Department's Defense Science Board noted, the

---

[6] David Sanger, "U.S. Hopes Face-Saving Plan Offers a Path to a Nuclear Pact With Iran," *The New York Times*, September 19, 2014. (http://www.nytimes.com/2014/09/20/world/middleeast/us-hopes-face-saving-plan-offers-apath-to-a-nuclear-pact-with-iran-.html?_r=0)

[7] Olli Heinonen, "Key Limitations on Iran's Uranium Enrichment Program," *Iran Task Force*, October 2014. (http://taskforceoniran.org/pdf/Enrichment_Memo.pdf)

[8] Among other references to Iran's ballistic missile capabilities, U.N. Security Council Resolution 1929 of June 2010 states, "Iran shall not undertake any activity related to ballistic missiles capable of delivering nuclear weapons, including launches using ballistic missile technology, and that States shall take all necessary measures to prevent the transfer of technology or technical assistance to Iran related to such activities." United Nations, Press Release, "Security Council Imposes Additional Sanctions on Iran, Voting 12 in Favour to 2 Against, with 1 Abstention Brazil, Turkey, Lebanon Say Tehran Declaration Could Boost Diplomatic Efforts, While Sanctions Represent Failure of Diplomacy," June 9, 2010. (http://www.un.org/News/Press/docs/2010/sc9948.doc.htm)

[9] Wendy Sherman, "House Foreign Affairs Committee Holds Hearing on Iran Nuclear Negotiations," *Testimony before the House Foreign Affairs Committee*, July 29, 2014. (accessed via Congressional Quarterly)

verification and inspection mechanisms "accounting for warheads instead of delivery platforms" are "inadequate."[10]

The P5+1 also appears willing to defer consideration of possible military dimensions (PMD) of Iran's military-nuclear program until after the conclusion of a comprehensive agreement. International Atomic Energy Agency Director General Yukiya Amano has been clear that Iran has not cooperated with the IAEA to resolve outstanding issues of concern related to Iran's past (and possibly ongoing) weaponization activities.[11] A September 2014 IAEA report revealed that Iran has failed to implement the preliminary, incremental steps it promised to the IAEA.[12] It seems unlikely that a final deal will require Iran to fully address these concerns. The likely scenario is that the P5+1 would set up a structure of phased sanctions relief calibrated to Iran's resolution of outstanding IAEA concerns.

This is a mistake: Without resolving these PMD issues, the IAEA will not easily establish an effective monitoring, verification, and inspection regime to ensure that Iran's nuclear activities are entirely peaceful. The IAEA cannot determine how far along Iran was on the path to nuclear weapons, where this activity took place, and who was involved. It is also unrealistic to assume that Iran, which failed to come clean on its weaponization activities when Western economic leverage was at its height, will be more forthcoming after a deal is signed. At that point, the euphoria of a diplomatic achievement, coupled with the provision of sanctions relief not linked to the satisfaction of the IAEA's concerns, will continue to strengthen Iran's economic recovery while providing additional leverage to Iran's leadership to resist IAEA demands. Indeed, the assumption that sanctions relief can be carefully calibrated to Iranian nuclear behavior – with an overreliance on the rapid reimplementation of sanctions in the event of Iranian non-compliance, could prove to be a fundamental flaw in the nuclear agreement (see below).

For these and other reasons, there is cause to fear that if a comprehensive agreement is reached between the P5+1 and Iran, it will not adequately prevent Iran's uranium and plutonium pathways to a nuclear weapon, address Iran's ability to develop long-range ballistic missiles capable of carrying nuclear warheads, and provide an adequate monitoring, verification, and inspection regime.

As a result, the more flawed the nuclear deal, the more important it will be to maintain sanctions as a critical instrument of deterrence and punishment for Iranian non-

---

[10] U.S. Department of Defense, Defense Science Board, "Assessment of Nuclear Monitoring and Verification Technologies," January 2014, page ii.
(http://www.acq.osd.mil/dsb/re\ports/NuclearMonitoringAndVerificationTechnologies.pdf)
[11] Jay Solomon, "Iran Blocks Inspections, Hobbling Nuclear Deal," *The Wall Street Journal*, October 31, 2014; (http://online.wsj.com/articles/iran-blocks-inspections-hobbling-nuclear-deal-1414797490) &
"Challenges in Nuclear Verification: The IAEA's Role on the Iranian Nuclear Issue," *Brookings Institution*, October 31, 2014. (http://www.brookings.edu/events/2014/10/31-challenge-nuclear-verification-iran-iaea-amano)
[12] International Atomic Energy Agency, "Implementation of the NPT Safeguards Agreement and Relevant Provisions of Security Council Resolutions in the Islamic Republic of Iran," September 5, 2014. (http://isis-online.org/uploads/isis-reports/documents/gov-2014-43.pdf)

compliance; as a vital enforcement mechanism to support a monitoring, verification, and inspection regime; and as a tool to curb Iran's support for terrorism and its abuse of human rights – two other issues that a nuclear deal with Iran will not address.

If a comprehensive agreement falls short of important parameters and allows Iran to retain essential elements of its military-nuclear infrastructure, Congress can and should defend the sanctions architecture that brought Iran to the negotiating table. Congress designed many of the toughest sanctions against Iran, and it will be vital for Congress to defend this core sanctions architecture to maintain essential economic leverage. Without it, the administration cannot effectively enforce the terms of the deal or punish Iranian non-compliance.

THE ADMINISTRATION'S PLAN TO CIRCUMVENT CONGRESS

The New York Times revealed in October that the administration has studied the issue of how the president might suspend the "vast majority" of sanctions while bypassing Congress.[13] According to one unnamed senior administration official: "We wouldn't seek congressional legislation in any comprehensive agreement for years. The early suspensions would be executive action."[14]

The approach likely would rely on a series of national security or national interest waivers, special rules, exemptions, licensing provisions, sunsets, and other tools that could be used at the president's discretion to cancel investigations or not enforce sanctions contained in Iran sanctions legislation (Iran Sanctions Act (ISA), Comprehensive Iran Sanctions, Accountability, and Divestment Act (CISADA), Section 1245 of the 2012 National Defense Authorization Act (NDAA), and Iran Freedom and Counter-Proliferation Act (IFCA)). The president could also terminate, suspend, or amend key executive orders that are not codified in legislation (and therefore not linked to legislative termination criteria), such as Executive Orders 13224, 13382, 13553, 13574, and 13628. Specifically, he could unilaterally suspend or terminate the designation of Iranian entities on Treasury's Specially Designated Nationals (SDN) list that are not codified under legislation.[15] For a guide to how the administration may do this, I recommend looking at the unwinding of U.S. sanctions on Burma.[16]

Should he embrace this approach, the president would be rejecting the advice of many members of this committee and 344 members of the House of Representatives who, in a

---

[13] David Sanger, "Obama Sees an Iran Deal That Could Avoid Congress," *The New York Times*, October 20, 2014. (http://www.nytimes.com/2014/10/20/us/politics/obama-sees-an-iran-deal-that-could-avoid-congress-.html?_r=1)

[14] David Sanger, "Lawmakers Express Skepticism on Iran Nuclear Deal," *The New York Times*, July 29, 2014. (http://www.nytimes.com/2014/07/30/world/middleeast/lawmakers-voice-skepticism-on-iran-nuclear-deal.html)

[15] For an analysis of how the Obama administration would suspend Iran sanctions, see a forthcoming paper from Jordan Chandler Hirsch & Matthew Blumenthal, Yale Law School.

[16] Michael F. Martin, "U.S. Sanctions on Burma," *Congressional Research Service*, October 19, 2012. (http://fpc.state.gov/documents/organization/200048.pdf); see also a forthcoming paper from Jordan Chandler Hirsch & Matthew Blumenthal, Yale Law School.

July 2014 letter to the president, underscored the importance of adhering to the termination criteria in CISADA and Iran Threat Reduction and Syria Human Rights Act of 2012 (ITRA) on the full range of Iran's illicit activities, not just its nuclear program: "Iran's permanent and verifiable termination of all these activities – not just some – is a prerequisite for permanently lifting most congressionally-mandated sanctions."[17] The letter also emphasized that "the concept of an exclusively defined 'nuclear related' sanction on Iran does not exist in U.S. law." Indeed, "almost all sanctions related to Iran's nuclear program are also related to Tehran's advancing ballistic missile program, intensifying support for international terrorism, and other unconventional weapons programs."[18]

Sanctions Termination Criteria

U.S. law links the termination of many of the most punitive financial and energy sanctions against Iran to specific criteria set out in the CISADA,[19] and modified by ITRA.[20] They require the president to certify to Congress that Iran has "ceased providing support for acts of international terrorism and no longer satisfies the requirements for designation as a state sponsor of terrorism," and that Iran has "ceased the pursuit, acquisition, and development, and verifiably dismantled its nuclear, biological, and chemical weapons and ballistic missiles and ballistic missile launch technology."[21]

It seems highly unlikely that any deal under consideration will meet these termination criteria. For example, press reports indicate that Iran's sponsorship of terrorism is not within the scope of the deal being negotiated and any agreement on ballistic missiles is unlikely to address all aspects of Iran's missile development.[22]

---

[17] House Committee on Foreign Affairs, Press Release, "342 House Members Join Chairman Royce, Ranking Member Engel in Calling on President Obama to Consult Congress on Iran Nuclear Negotiations," July 10, 2014. (http://foreignaffairs.house.gov/press-release/342-house-members-join-chairman-royce-ranking-member-engel-calling-president-obama)

[18] House Committee on Foreign Affairs, Press Release, "342 House Members Join Chairman Royce, Ranking Member Engel in Calling on President Obama to Consult Congress on Iran Nuclear Negotiations," July 10, 2014. (http://foreignaffairs.house.gov/press-release/342-house-members-join-chairman-royce-ranking-member-engel-calling-president-obama)

[19] U.S. House of Representatives, 111th Congress, 2nd Session, P.L. 111-195, "Comprehensive Iran Sanctions, Accountability, and Divestment Act of 2010," Section 401, *Government Printing Office*, 2010, page 40. (http://www.treasury.gov/resource-center/sanctions/Documents/hr2194.pdf)

[20] U.S. House of Representatives, 112th Congress, 2nd Session, H.R. 1905, "Iran Threat Reduction and Syria Human Rights Act of 2012," *Government Printing Office*. 2012. (http://www.gpo.gov/fdsys/pkg/BILLS-112hr1905enr/pdf/BILLS-112hr1905enr.pdf)

[21] U.S. House of Representatives, 111th Congress, 2nd Session, P.L. 111-195, "Comprehensive Iran Sanctions, Accountability, and Divestment Act of 2010," Section 401, *Government Printing Office*, 2010, page 40. (http://www.treasury.gov/resource-center/sanctions/Documents/hr2194.pdf)

[22] Armin Rosen, "Obama Sent A Letter To Iran's Supreme Leader Tying The ISIS Fight To A Nuclear Deal," *Business Insider*, November 6, 2014; (http://www.businessinsider.com/r-obama-sent-secret-letter-to-iran-on-fighting-islamic-state-wsj-2014-11) & Wendy Sherman, "House Foreign Affairs Committee Holds Hearing on Iran Nuclear Negotiations," *Testimony before the House Foreign Affairs Committee*, July 29, 2014. (accessed via Congressional Quarterly)

It also seems improbable that a final agreement regarding Iran's nuclear program will resolve all of the money laundering and illicit finance concerns, particularly those related to the Central Bank of Iran (CBI). The U.S. imposed sanctions on the Central Bank of Iran pursuant to Section 1245 of the National Defense Authorization Act (NDAA) for Fiscal Year 2012. These sanctions were premised on the Central Bank's involvement in money laundering, terror finance, and weapons proliferation.[23] To date, the administration has not rescinded its USA PATRIOT Act Section 311 finding with respect to Iran, which found the entire Iranian financial system, including its Central Bank, to be a threat to the international financial system.[24]

Conduct-Based Financial Sanctions

The Obama administration has recognized that the Iran sanctions regime is designed to respond to the full range of Iran's dangerous activities. As U.S. Treasury Under Secretary David Cohen explained, a primary goal of the sanctions on Iran is to "protect the integrity of the U.S. and international financial systems" from illicit finance.[25] Following five years of individual designations of Iranian and foreign financial institutions for involvement in illicit finance supporting weapons proliferation and terrorism,[26] Treasury issued a finding under Section 311 of the USA PATRIOT Act that Iran is a "jurisdiction of primary money laundering concern."[27] Treasury cited Iran's "support for terrorism," "pursuit of weapons of mass destruction," and use of "deceptive financial practices to facilitate illicit conduct and evade sanctions."[28]

---

[23] U.S. House of Representatives, 112th Congress, 1st Session, P.L. 112-81, "National Defense Authorization Act for Fiscal Year 2012," Section 1245: Imposition of Sanctions With Respect to the Financial Sector of Iran, *Government Printing Office*, 2011, page 350. (http://www.gpo.gov/fdsys/pkg/BILLS-112hr1540enr/pdf/BILLS-112hr1540enr.pdf)

[24] David S. Cohen, "The Entire Iranian Banking Sector," *U.S. Department of the Treasury*, November 22, 2011. (http://www.treasury.gov/connect/blog/Pages/The-Entire-Iranian-Banking-Sector.aspx)

[25] . David Cohen, "Remarks of Under Secretary for Terrorism and Financial Intelligence David Cohen Before the New York University School of Law on 'The Law and Policy of Iran Sanctions'," *New York University School of Law*, September 12, 2012. (http://www.treasury.gov/press-center/press-releases/Pages/tg1706.aspx)

[26] Treasury designated 23 Iranian and Iranian-allied foreign financial institutions as "proliferation supporting entities" under Executive Order 13382 and sanctioned Bank Saderat as a "terrorism supporting entity" under Executive Order 13224. At least eight of the sanctioned banks were designated for their ties to Iran's Islamic Revolutionary Guard Corps (IRGC) or because they were controlled by banks with IRGC links: Bank Sepah (Iran); Bank Melli (Iran); Arian Bank (Iran); Bank Kargoshaee (Iran), controlled by Bank Melli; Future Bank (Bahrain), controlled by Bank Melli; Post Bank of Iran (Iran), controlled by Bank Sepah; Ansar Bank (Iran); Mehr Bank (Iran). U.S. Department of the Treasury, Press Release, "Treasury Cuts Iran's Bank Saderat Off from U.S. Financial System," September 8, 2006; (http://www.treasury.gov/press-center/press-releases/Pages/hp87.aspx) & U.S. Department of the Treasury, Press Release, "Treasury Designates Major Iranian State-Owned Bank," January 23, 2012. (http://www.treasury.gov/press-center/press-releases/Pages/tg1397.aspx)

[27] U.S. Department of the Treasury, Press Release, "Finding That the Islamic Republic of Iran is a Jurisdiction of Primary Money Laundering Concern," November 18, 2011. (http://www.treasury.gov/press-center/press-releases/Documents/Iran311Finding.pdf)

[28] U.S. Department of the Treasury, Press Release, "Finding That the Islamic Republic of Iran is a Jurisdiction of Primary Money Laundering Concern," November 18, 2011. (http://www.treasury.gov/press-center/press-releases/Documents/Iran311Finding.pdf)

Treasury targeted the CBI and made it clear that the entire country's financial system posed "illicit finance risks for the global financial system."[29] The Financial Action Task Force (FATF), an international body comprised of 34 members plus the European Commission and the Gulf Co-operation Council,[30] reaffirmed this concern by warning its members that they should, "advise their financial institutions to give special attention to business relationships and transactions with Iran, including Iranian companies and financial institutions," and to, "apply effective counter-measures to protect their financial sectors from money laundering and financing of terrorism (ML/FT) risks emanating from Iran."[31]

Because the Section 311 finding is conduct-based, the lifting of this action should be dependent on specific changes in the full range of Iran's illicit finance activities. However, Washington has, in the past, made the mistake of giving "bad banks" access to the global financial system in order to secure a nuclear agreement.

In 2005, Treasury issued a Section 311 finding against Macau-based Banco Delta Asia,[32] and within days, North Korean accounts and transactions were frozen or blocked in banking capitals around the world. However, facing a North Korean negotiating team that refused to make nuclear concessions before sanctions relief and a North Korean regime, which had defiantly conducted its first nuclear test,[33] the State Department advocated for the release of frozen North Korean funds on good faith.[34] The State Department ultimately prevailed, and Chinese and other banks renewed their financial relationships with Pyongyang. Washington lost its leverage and its credibility by divorcing the Section 311 finding from the illicit conduct that had prompted the designation in the first place. Undeterred, North Korea moved forward with its nuclear weapons program, not to mention money laundering, counterfeiting, and other financial crimes.

Compromising the integrity of the U.S. and global financial system to conclude a limited agreement with North Korea neither sealed the deal nor protected the system. There are concerns that we might see a repetition of this cycle with Iran if financial restrictions are lifted without certifications that Iran's illicit finance activities have ceased.

CONGRESSIONAL DEFENSE OF THE SANCTIONS ARCHITECTURE

---

[29] U.S. Department of the Treasury, Press Release, "Fact Sheet: New Sanctions on Iran," November 21, 2011. (http://www.treasury.gov/press-center/press-releases/Pages/tg1367.aspx)

[30] A list of the members of FATF can be found FATF's website. "FATF Members and Observers," *Financial Action Task Force Website*, accessed June 23, 2014. (http://www.fatf-gafi.org/pages/aboutus/membersandobservers/)

[31] The Financial Action Task Force, Public Statement, "FATF Public Statement 14 February 2014." February 14, 2014. (http://www.fatf-gafi.org/countries/d-i/islamicrepublicofiran/documents/public-statement-feb-2014.html)

[32] . U.S. Department of the Treasury, Press Release, "Treasury Designates Banco Delta Asia as Primary Money Laundering Concern Under USA PATRIOT Act," September 15, 2005. (http://www.treasury.gov/press-center/press-releases/Pages/js2720.aspx)

[33] David E. Sanger, "North Koreans Say They Tested Nuclear Device," *The New York Times*, October 9, 2006. (http://www.nytimes.com/2006/10/09/world/asia/09korea.html?pagewanted=all)

[34] Juan Zarate, *Treasury's War: The Unleashing of a New Era of Financial Warfare*, (New York: Public Affairs, 2013), page 258.

Congress should defend the core sanctions architecture, based on the following principles:

- preserving core elements of the financial and energy sanctions architecture until Iran has ended all forms of illicit activity, since rebuilding that architecture and regaining international buy-in would be extremely challenging;

- recognizing the inherent asymmetry between the reciprocal concessions provided as part of a comprehensive agreement. Indeed, it may be more difficult for the P5+1 to re-impose sanctions in a timely manner in the event of Iranian non-compliance than it will be for Iran to re-start or construct key elements of its nuclear and ballistic missile infrastructure;

- providing the United States and its P5+1 partners with sufficient economic leverage through the maintenance of specific sanctions after an agreement is signed to deter and commensurately punish Iranian non-compliance. This will provide leverage to support a monitoring, verification, and inspection regime, and provide a mechanism for U.S. unilateral and third-party sanctions to penalize Iran if Iran violates the terms of the agreement;

- maintaining the original-stated rationale for the sanctions against Iran, particularly the financial sanctions designed to protect the integrity of the global financial system from the illicit activities of Iranian entities; and,

- reaffirming sanctions related to terrorism and human rights to support the Obama administration's stated policy that terrorism and human rights sanctions are distinct from "nuclear-related sanctions" and therefore not precluded as a result of any agreement. This will ensure that, after a long-term agreement on the status of Iran's nuclear program is reached, the United States continues to pressure Iran to end its support for global terrorism, active support for the Bashar al-Assad regime in Syria, and its vast system of domestic repression at home.

In order to prevent the provision of sanctions relief in advance of Iran meeting specific, verifiable nuclear and illicit finance benchmarks, Congress can provide rigorous oversight of all sanctions relief, legislate objective criteria that must be met before relief can be provided, and lay out specific punishments for Iranian non-compliance with the agreement.

Congress should request a clear definition from the Obama administration and the P5+1 partners on what constitutes a breach of the nuclear agreement, particularly in light of Iran's track record of nuclear non-compliance. For example, according to David Albright and his colleagues at the Institute for Science and International Studies, in analyzing a recent November IAEA report, Iran has fed uranium into an advanced centrifuge, going beyond the advanced centrifuge research and development permitted under the JPOA and thus violating the terms of JPOA.[35]

There is ample reason for concern that the P5+1 may not effectively respond to Iranian non-compliance given the complexities of detection, Iranian obfuscation, and the political and bureaucratic challenges (coordinating between the IAEA, P5+1 and within the U.S. government) in getting firm agreement over whether non-compliance occurred and determining the appropriate response. There may be a tendency for senior administration officials to not respond effectively to evidence of Iranian non-compliance out of fear that vigorous enforcement could lead to Iranian countermeasures. This may be particularly problematic when Congress is concerned about reports of a growing U.S.-Iran détente and possible American-Iranian coordination to weaken the Islamic State.[36] As a result, Congress should assert and act on its prerogative to provide oversight on what would constitute a material breach of the agreement.

The Psychology Versus the Legalities of "Snapbacks"

Based on press reports, it appears that the Obama administration is designing a phased-program of sanctions relief using "suspensions" and "snapbacks" where sanctions will be suspended and then re-imposed in the event of Iranian non-compliance.[37] This approach may also be adopted by the European Union. It may also potentially be used to deal with the U.N. Security Council Resolutions and related sanctions.

The legalities of snapbacks are relatively simple. In the U.S., the Obama administration could decide unilaterally, on evidence of Iranian non-compliance, to immediately re-impose any of the suspended sanctions. In the European Union, where the *imposition* of sanctions requires the support of all 28 members of the EU, sanctions could be suspended temporarily, for example every 180 days, with a vote necessary to *renew the suspension*, and thus a veto by only one member state would reinstate the sanctions. A similar mechanism could be used at the U.N. Security Council, where a renewal of the suspension of the U.N. Security Council Resolutions could be blocked by one UNSC permanent member. This would effectively give France, for example, a veto over the renewal of the suspension of sanctions in the EU and the United States, France, or the U.K. a veto over the continued suspension of sanctions at the UNSC.

---

[35] David Albright, Paulina Izewicz, Andrea Stricker, and Serena Kelleher-Vergantini, "ISIS Analysis of IAEA Iran Safeguards Report," *Institute for Science and International Security*, November 7, 2014, pages 1 & 3. (http://isis-online.org/uploads/isis-reports/documents/ISIS_Analysis_IAEA_Report_7Nov2014-Final.pdf)

[36] Jay Solomon & Carol E. Lee, "Obama Wrote Secret Letter to Iran's Khamenei About Fighting Islamic State," *The Wall Street Journal*, November 6, 2014; (http://online.wsj.com/articles/obama-wrote-secret-letter-to-irans-khamenei-about-fighting-islamic-state-1415295291) Michael R. Crittenden & Carol E. Lee, "Obama's Letter to Iran Rattles Congressional Nerves," *The Wall Street Journal*, November 6, 2014; (http://blogs.wsj.com/washwire/2014/11/06/obamas-letter-to-iran-rattles-congressional-nerves/) & Jay Solomon & Maria Abi-Habib, "U.S., Iran Relations Move to Détente," *The Wall Street Journal*, October 28, 2014. (http://online.wsj.com/articles/u-s-iran-relations-move-to-detente-1414539659)

[37] David Sanger, "Obama Sees an Iran Deal That Could Avoid Congress," *The New York Times*, October 20, 2014. (http://www.nytimes.com/2014/10/20/us/politics/obama-sees-an-iran-deal-that-could-avoid-congress-.html?_r=1)

The politics and economics of snapbacks are more complicated. Politically, at the U.S., EU, and UNSC levels, respectively, there would have to be agreement that there is sufficient evidence of Iranian non-compliance to warrant a decision to reinstate the sanctions. There are bound to be significant disputes on the evidence, differing assessments of the seriousness of infractions, fierce debates about the appropriate level of response, and concerns about Iranian retaliation. The snapback is equally challenging to implement given the economic realities that will follow a nuclear deal. International sanctions took years before a critical mass of international companies terminated their business ties with Tehran. Once loosened, with so many international companies positioning to get back into Iran,[38] it will be difficult to persuade these companies to leave again, especially as Western companies, and their lobby groups, will argue that Chinese, Russian, Turkish, and other less cooperative countries are bound to backfill if they do.

The Iranian regime also is likely to take steps to minimize its economic exposure when it anticipates that it will violate any nuclear agreement. For example, it may move its oil revenues out of Western bank accounts into accounts held in jurisdictions less exposed to U.S. pressure; this will diminish the impact of a snapback of the oil-revenue escrow restrictions, which may be a preferred way for the Obama administration to maintain some economic leverage. Finally, as discussed below, Iran will enjoy substantial psychological benefits from the deal that will translate into improved macroeconomic conditions – as it already has under the JPOA.[39]

The Psychology Versus the Legalities of Sanctions

An overreliance on "snapback" sanctions can be problematic since the impact of the underlying sanctions is as much psychological as legal. The efficacy of sanctions is predicated upon a strategy of escalation and the perception of high risk. An ever-expanding web of restrictions effectively spooked foreign businesses from investing in, or trading with, Iran. During the period of sanctions escalation, fear triumphed over greed as companies viewed Iran as an economic minefield, and Iranian investors and consumers lost confidence in their economy. Unfortunately, the JPOA began to reverse this phenomenon. As FDD's economic research has shown,[40] the Obama administration's estimates of the value of direct sanctions relief provided by the JPOA did not account for

---

[38] Jay Solomon, "Oil, Auto Companies Make Plans to Invest in Iran if Sanctions Ease," *The Wall Street Journal*, July 1, 2014; (http://online.wsj.com/articles/oil-auto-companies-make-plans-to-invest-in-iran-if-sanctions-ease-1404257812) & Saeed Kamali Dehghan, "Iranians and Multinationals Hungry For Nuclear Deal That Will End Sanctions," *The Guardian* (U.K.), November 14, 2014.
(http://www.theguardian.com/world/2014/nov/14/iranians-multinationals-hungry-nuclear-deal-to-end-sanctions)

[39] Paul Domjan, Mark Dubowitz, Jennifer Hsieh, & Rachel Ziemba, "Sanctions Relief: What Did Iran Get?," *Foundation for Defense of Democracies & Roubini Global Economics*, July 2014.
(http://defenddemocracy.org/content/uploads/general/RoubiniFDDReport.pdf)

[40] Paul Domjan, Mark Dubowitz, Jennifer Hsieh, & Rachel Ziemba, "Sanctions Relief: What Did Iran Get?," *Foundation for Defense of Democracies & Roubini Global Economics*, July 2014.
(http://defenddemocracy.org/content/uploads/general/RoubiniFDDReport.pdf)

the psychological impact on markets, business, and investors and the broader impact on Iran's macroeconomic environment.

Using a proprietary sentiment indicator developed by Roubini Global Economics, in partnership with the Foundation for Defense of Democracies,[41] we have tracked the economic impact of the de-escalation of sanctions (since mid-2013), the optimism surrounding the election of President Rouhani (June 2013), the announcement of the JPOA agreement (November 2013), the announcement of the JPOA implementation agreement (January 2014), and the subsequent direct sanctions relief. The indicator identified a change in the perceptions of Iran globally and perhaps more importantly within Iran itself, where confidence in the rial's value increased, making Iranians more confident to hold domestic assets rather than hoarding dollars or fuelling domestic asset bubbles. This, in turn, gave breathing space to the Iranian government to put its economy on a stronger foundation by tightening fiscal and monetary policy to restrain inflation.

As a result, the Iranian economy has shown signs of modest growth and stabilization. There has been an undeniable shift in market psychology, both among Iranian businesses and those companies angling to do business with Iran. The change in Iranian consumer and investor sentiment has boosted Iran's economic performance, as reflected in modest GDP growth, a stabilization of Iran's currency, and a significant drop in inflation.[42]

Indeed, Iran has been on a modest recovery path since its *annus horribilis* of 2012 and the first half of 2013, when the Iranian economy was hit with an asymmetric shock from sanctions targeting: the Central Bank of Iran, Iranian oil exports, access to the SWIFT international banking system, the National Iranian Oil Company, shipping and insurance, key sectors of the Iranian economy, including energy, shipping and shipbuilding, and precious metals, among others. The poor economic management of the Iranian economy by the Mahmoud Ahmadinejad government further exacerbated these sanctions-induced shocks. Since the election of Hassan Rouhani as Iran's president in June 2013, a more competent economic team, under less severe sanctions-induced economic stress than its predecessors, has implemented more effective monetary and fiscal policies, which have increased the durability of Iran's recovery.

As Iran's economic recovery becomes more durable, and less susceptible to snapback sanctions, economic pressure will diminish as an effective tool to respond to Iranian nuclear non-compliance. This will make it more likely that the U.S. will be forced to choose between either tolerating Iranian cheating or using more coercive means, including military force, to enforce the deal and prevent it from unraveling.

RECOMMENDATIONS

---

[41] Mark Dubowitz & Paul Domjan. "New Sentiment Indicator Shows Positive Impact of Sanctions Relief on Iran's Economy," *Foundation for Defense of Democracies & Roubini Global Economics*, May 15, 2014. (http://www.defenddemocracy.org/content/uploads/documents/Final_Sentiment_Report.pdf)

[42] Jennifer Hsieh, Rachel Ziemba, & Mark Dubowitz, "Iran's Economy, Out of the Red, Slowly Growing." *Foundation for Defense of Democracies & Roubini Global Economics*, October 2014. (http://defenddemocracy.org/content/uploads/publications/RoubiniFDDReport_Oct14.pdf)

Since sanctions snapbacks will be difficult to implement politically and economically, Congress needs to defend the sanctions architecture in a way that is not overly reliant on mechanisms to re-impose sanctions; the snapback has a role to play (as noted below) but only in the context of a comprehensive sanctions relief program where core elements of the sanctions are maintained. Congress should consider adopting the following recommendations into a sanctions defense, enforcement, and relief bill to preserve American economic leverage.[43] This leverage will be critical to the enforcement of a nuclear deal with an Iranian regime that has a decades-long track record of nuclear mendacity, and a long rap sheet of terrorist activities and financial crimes.

Financial Sector Sanctions

While U.S. financial sanctions are implemented and enforced by the U.S. Treasury Department, Congress can play a crucial role by legislating the terms of a rehabilitation program for designated Iranian banks and by laying out specific benchmarks that must be met prior to the suspension of financial sanctions.

1. **Develop a rehabilitation program for designated Iranian banks that puts the onus on Tehran to demonstrate that the banks are no longer engaged in illicit financial conduct.**

As part of sanctions relief, the P5+1 may agree to the suspension of sanctions against specific Iranian banks. While Treasury will ultimately be responsible for U.S. designations, Congress can and should lay out criteria for de-designation and for re-designation if a bank re-engages in illicit financial activities.

Congress should require that Treasury submit a financial sanctions rehabilitation program plan and mandate that specific benchmarks be met before Treasury can suspend the designations of qualifying banks. This legislation could include snapback provisions that will immediately re-designate banks that engage in illicit financial transactions. As an additional deterrent against banned activity, all re-designated banks would permanently lose the right to qualify for rehabilitation and be permanently banned from the U.S. financial system and SWIFT (assuming EU agreement). Congress could also amend CISADA and Section 1245 of the FY2012 NDAA to ensure that any foreign financial institution transacting with a permanently banned Iranian bank would be automatically subject to penalties, including losing correspondent banking relationships with U.S. financial institutions. Congress should also require Treasury to include a certification, subject to periodic reviews, that will be published in the Federal Register prior to de-designation.

Legislation should enable Congress to affirm or reject these certifications.

---

[43] Mark Dubowitz & Richard Goldberg, "Smart Relief after an Iran Deal," *Foundation for Defense of Democracies*, June 2014. (http://www.defenddemocracy.org/content/uploads/documents/Final_Smart_Sanctions_Report.pdf)

2. Legislate criteria for the suspension of sanctions on the Central Bank of Iran and the lifting of the Section 311 finding against the entire Iranian financial system.

The suspension of sanctions against CBI, even more than the de-designation of individual Iranian banks, would provide significant relief to Iran and should therefore also be tied to verifiable changes in Iranian behavior. Before suspending the statutory designation of the CBI under Section 1245 of the FY2012 NDAA, the president should be required to provide certifications to Congress. Lawmakers could require the president to certify to Congress, prior to suspending sanctions against CBI, that Iran is no longer a "jurisdiction of primary money laundering concern" and that the CBI, as the central pillar of Iran's illicit financial activities, is no longer engaged in "support for terrorism," "pursuit of weapons of mass destruction," or any "illicit and deceptive financial activities." Congress could stipulate that Treasury must be confident that the entire country's financial system no longer poses "illicit finance risks for the global financial system." The legislation should also enable Congress to affirm or reject these certifications.

Finally, Congress should require a presidential certification that Iran is no longer a "jurisdiction of primary money laundering concern" prior to the suspension of the Section 311 finding against Iran's entire financial system. This would include the financing of terror groups, such as Hezbollah, Hamas, Palestinian Islamic Jihad, and others. Treasury could also be required to provide certification of its confidence that Iran no longer poses illicit finance risks for the global financial system. Again, legislation should enable Congress to affirm or reject this certification.

3. Tie gold sanctions relief to money laundering certifications

Iran's money laundering and sanctions evasion activities will remain a concern even after a potential nuclear agreement is reached. Therefore, Congress should pass legislation to amend the Iran Freedom and Counter-Proliferation Act (IFCA)[44] which was enacted as part of the FY2013 National Defense Authorization Act to require a presidential certification that the Iranian financial sector, including the CBI, is no longer a jurisdiction of primary money laundering concern prior to the suspension of precious metal sanctions. The amendment could also clarify that any temporary suspension will only become permanent when the president can provide certification that Iran is no longer a state sponsor of terrorism. Legislation should enable Congress to affirm or reject this certification.

Energy Sector Sanctions

Iran is under four main types of energy sanctions:

---

[44]. U.S. Department of State, "Fact Sheet: Iran Freedom and Counter-Proliferation Act of 2012," accessed June 25, 2014. (http://www.state.gov/documents/organization/208111.pdf)

a) Refined petroleum sanctions related to the domestic production and import of refined petroleum products (pursuant to the Iran Sanctions Act as modified by CISADA);

b) Investment and technology-related sanctions that have reduced Iran's petroleum production capacity (pursuant to ISA as modified by CISADA and provisions of ITRA);

c) Financial sanctions that curtail its ability to export its crude oil (pursuant to Section 1245 of the FY2012 NDAA) and access the crude oil revenues generated from those sales (pursuant to the "February 6" escrow provisions of ITRA[45]).

d) Sector-based sanctions (pursuant to the Iran Freedom and Counter Proliferation Act in the FY2013 NDAA).

Congress created these sanctions and the secondary sanctions. It should therefore play a leading role in determining how and when they can be suspended.

4. Legislate the "snapback" provisions and sunset terms of refined petroleum, investment, technology-related, and sector-based energy sanctions.

Under current legislation, the president is able to temporarily suspend the refined petroleum sanctions on Iran for twelve months pursuant to the national security interest waiver in CISADA.[46] This suspension has a significant impact on Iran's ability to import higher quality refined petroleum products from foreign suppliers, instead of relying on domestic substitutes that have contributed to pollution. Certain investments, technology-related sanctions, and sector-based energy sanctions can also be suspended for 180 days pursuant to the president's national security interest waiver authority – either through the Iran Sanctions Act or IFCA.[47]

For refined petroleum, investments, technology-related, and sector-based energy sanctions, Congress should legislate conditions for the "snapback" of any suspension of these sanctions to deter or punish Iranian non-compliance with the final agreement. Specifically, Congress should require that in order for the president to use and renew the national security waivers, he must certify that Iran is fulfilling its commitments under the comprehensive nuclear agreement and that no energy-related monies, technologies, goods, or services are being used in Iran's energy sector to support illicit proliferation

[45]. Kenneth Katzman, "Iran Sanctions," *Congressional Research Service*, May 7, 2014, page 22. (http://fas.org/sgp/crs/mideast/RS20871.pdf)

[46] A twelve month suspension is permissible under CISADA if the "government with primary jurisdiction over the person is closely cooperating with the United States in multilateral efforts to prevent Iran from acquiring weapons of mass destruction or advanced conventional weapons." U.S. House of Representatives, 111th Congress, 2nd Session, P.L. 111-195, "Comprehensive Iran Sanctions, Accountability, and Divestment Act of 2010," *Government Printing Office*, 2010, page 14. (http://www.treasury.gov/resource-center/sanctions/Documents/hr2194.pdf)

[47] U.S. Department of State, "Fact Sheet: Iran Freedom and Counter-Proliferation Act of 2012," accessed June 25, 2014. (http://www.state.gov/documents/organization/208111.pdf)

activities, terrorism or any financial crimes. If the president cannot make this certification, all energy sanctions should be re-imposed.

Legislation should enable Congress to affirm or reject these certifications.

Finally, Congress should be prepared to automatically renew the provisions of the Iran Sanctions Act for an additional five-year period, and override the president's authority to unilaterally allow the legislation to sunset, when it ceases to be effective on December 31, 2016.

5. **Protect Europe's crude oil embargo and the maintenance of current Iranian crude oil export levels by clarifying and strengthening exceptions to Section 1245 sanctions.**

During the JPOA negotiating period, the Obama administration has allowed the maintenance of Iran's crude oil export levels and has not sought "further reductions from the current purchasers of Iranian crude oil."[48] Therefore, under the JPOA, Iran has received substantial sanctions relief because further significant reductions in crude oil imports have not been mandated. Rather than this continued non-enforcement of the significant reduction requirements under FY2012 NDAA Section 1245, Congress could amend the legislation to allow for the maintenance of current levels of crude oil imports from Iran so long as Iran complies with the terms of the final nuclear agreement. This amendment of the legislation should also include a clarification that condensates are "counted" as part of the crude oil imports. During the JPOA period, as a concession to Iran, the Obama administration has permitted Iran unrestricted sales of condensates despite congressional interpretation of Section 1245 that condensates were also subject to the significant reduction requirements.[49]

Since Section 1245 is linked to the Central Bank of Iran's role in supporting terrorism and other financial crimes, Congress should clarify in legislation that Iran's oil buyers are not permitted to increase their imports of crude oil from Iran – or rather if they do, they may be subject to U.S. sanctions – until the president can certify that Iran is no longer a state sponsor of terrorism and the CBI and Iran's entire financial sector are no longer primary money laundering concerns. Legislation should enable Congress to affirm or reject this certification.

In addition to restricting the purchases of Iran's customers to current levels, these congressional actions will support Europe's crude oil embargo, which has had a serious impact on Iran's oil exports. The cumulative effect of U.S. and European sanctions reduced Iranian crude oil exports, which accounted for approximately 80 percent of

---

[48] U.S. Department of the Treasury, "Frequently Asked Questions Relating to the Extension of Temporary Sanctions Relief to Implement the Joint Plan of Action between the P5 + 1 and the Islamic Republic of Iran," July 21, 2014, page 7. (http://www.treasury.gov/resource-center/sanctions/Programs/Documents/jpoa_faqs_ext.pdf)

[49] Arshad Mohammed & Timothy Gardner, "Why Higher Iran Oil Exports Are Not Roiling Nuclear Deal," *Reuters*, June 12, 2014. (http://www.reuters.com/article/2014/06/12/us-iran-nuclear-oil-insight-idUSKBN0EN2GL20140612)

Iran's export earnings, from 2.5 million barrels per day to approximately 1 million.[50] Congressional legislation to clarify that any suspension of the significant reduction requirements does not also allow for the increase in imports or new customers could provide support for European countries to resist potential pressure from their EU partners to suspend or lift the embargo prematurely.

6. Legislate under what circumstances funds in escrow accounts can be released.

Oil revenues are currently accumulating in escrow accounts subject to the "February 6" restrictions of ITRA.[51] Iran can only spend these escrow funds on non-sanctionable goods, as defined under U.S. law, in the countries where they are accumulating (China, India, Japan, South Korea, Turkey, and Taiwan) or on humanitarian goods from a third country. The funds are accumulating in the escrow accounts because Tehran has not yet found enough goods in those counties that the government wants to purchase despite Japan's world-class pharmaceuticals industry, India's large generic drug industry, and South Korea's and Japan's sophisticated medical equipment production.

During the initial six months of the JPOA and the four-month extension, Iran has received $7 billion in installments from these escrow accounts. The funds have been released to the Iranian government to spend at its discretion. Under Secretary Cohen testified before the full committee of the House Foreign Affairs Committee that the U.S. Treasury "can't guarantee" that Iran is not using these funds to finance terrorism.[52]

As part of a comprehensive agreement or another extension of the interim agreement, the P5+1 may agree to release additional funds from the escrow accounts. Instead of allowing the repatriation of the funds to Iran, Congress should amend ITRA to create a mechanism for the release of specific amounts in installments if Iran is complying with its commitments. A payment plan could be tied to verifiable implementation of specific commitments under the agreement. This mechanism should ensure that the funds are being used for the purchase of non-sanctioned goods and not for illicit activities.

Congress could work with the Treasury Department to provide for the transfer of the escrow funds to a select few qualified foreign banks (for example, in Europe from where Iran could import goods and services), as determined by the Treasury Department. Iran could then have access to these oil revenues for the purposes of purchasing unlimited amounts of non-sanctionable goods, as defined under U.S. law, from the country where the qualifying bank is domiciled. These funds would not be permitted to be used for third-country, non-humanitarian trade but could be used to purchase humanitarian goods from any trading partner.

---

[50] "Sanctions Reduced Iran's Oil Exports and Revenues in 2012," *U.S. Energy Information Administration*, April 26, 2013. (http://www.eia.gov/todayinenergy/detail.cfm?id=11011)

[51] Kenneth Katzman, "Iran Sanctions," *Congressional Research Service*, May 7, 2014, page 22. (http://fas.org/sgp/crs/mideast/RS20871.pdf)

[52] David Cohen, "House Foreign Affairs Committee Holds Hearing on Iran Nuclear Negotiations," *Testimony before the House Foreign Affairs Committee*, July 29, 2014. (accessed via Congressional Quarterly)

As part of the amendment to ITRA, Congress could clarify that none of these escrowed oil funds can be repatriated back to Iran until Treasury certifies that Iran is no longer a "primary money laundering concern" or a state sponsor of terrorism.

Legislation should enable Congress to affirm or reject these certifications.

7. Work with the administration on licenses provided to those transacting business or other activities with Iran

Congress also needs greater insight into the administration's ability to license certain transactions under both its executive orders, including in codified legislation, and under the International Emergency Economic Powers Act (IEEPA) authorities. Congress needs to know who is receiving licenses for doing business in Iran – from general licenses to specific licenses – and for what purposes. In addition to the de-designation processes for SDNs, including Iranian financial institutions, this is another way that the administration may provide select relief to Iran, relatively free of congressional oversight. Congress should require presidential certifications for any license granted and legislation should enable Congress to affirm or reject these certifications.

Other Sanctions

Press reports indicate that the terms of any final agreement are unlikely to address outstanding concerns regarding Iran's support for terrorism, threatening and destabilizing behavior towards its neighbors, and systematic human rights abuses. As such, Congress should clarify that no sanctions relief will go to Iran's Islamic Revolutionary Guard Corps (IRGC) or IRGC-affiliated entities. Terrorism and human rights sanctions should also be strengthened and expanded if the behavior underlying these sanctions continues. This is in keeping with the Obama administration's insistence that the negotiations only cover "nuclear-related sanctions" and that as a matter of policy, terrorism and human rights sanctions will continue to be enforced.[53]

8. Reinforce certifications for suspensions of sector-based sanctions.

In addition to imposing sector-wide energy sanctions, IFCA also designated Iran's shipping, shipbuilding, and port operator sectors. The legislation further prohibited the transfer of goods and services to such sectors, and the sale, supply, or transfer of various

---

[53] For example, Jake Sullivan, then-national security adviser to Vice President Biden and deputy assistant to President Obama and current senior advisor to the U.S. government and participant in the P5+1 negotiations said, "We have made clear that sanctions relating to terrorism and sanctions relating to human rights violations are not covered by the discussions that we are having on the nuclear file ... I can tell you, as a matter of policy this administration is committed to continuing to enforce and follow through on that set of sanctions." Jake Sullivan, "Washington Forum: A Conversation with Jake Sullivan, Deputy Assistant to President Obama and National Security Adviser to Vice President Joe Biden," *Foundation for Defense of Democracies Washington Forum 2014*, May 1, 2014.
(http://www.defenddemocracy.org/stuff/uploads/documents/SullivanFinal_transcript_WF14.pdf)

metals and materials to blacklisted sectors, individuals, and any sector determined to be linked to the IRGC.[54]

Congress should clarify that any suspension of these sector-based sanctions requires a presidential certification that each sector is not linked to the IRGC or involved in supporting terrorism or other illicit activities as stipulated under U.S. law. Congress could specify that the certification must be renewed every six months, and if the president cannot make the certification for a given sector, those sanctions would immediately snap back into effect. Legislation should enable Congress to affirm or reject these certifications.

9. Enforce and expand designations of IRGC-affiliated entities.

Designating entities and individuals in order to implement existing sanctions, including sanctions against the IRGC, is permitted under the JPOA. In August, the Treasury and State Departments announced the imposition of sanctions including "targeting Iran's missile and nuclear programs, sanctions evasion efforts, and support for terrorism."[55]

Congress could also clarify that designations will continue and that no sanctions, whether based on the IRGC's nuclear, ballistic missile, or terrorism activities, will be lifted against any entity or financial institution specifically designated because of its connection to the IRGC unless, and until, the president certifies that Iran is no longer a state sponsor of terrorism and the IRGC no longer meets the criteria as a designated entity under U.S. law. Legislation should enable Congress to affirm or reject these certifications.

As my colleagues at FDD, Emanuele Ottolenghi and Saeed Ghasseminejad, have argued, sanctioning IRGC entities and targeting the IRGC's "economic empire" will "weaken those inside Iran who are most likely to oppose a deal and seek to sabotage it."[56]

10. Enforce and expand terrorism- and human rights-related designations.

Iran's continued support for global terrorism requires that U.S. terrorism sanctions be maintained and expanded, notwithstanding any nuclear deal. Currently, Iran is subject to a wide range of terrorism-related sanctions imposed through both executive orders and

---

[54] U.S. Department of State, "Fact Sheet: Iran Freedom and Counter-Proliferation Act of 2012," accessed June 25, 2014. (http://www.state.gov/documents/organization/208111.pdf)

[55] U.S. Department of the Treasury, Press Release, "Treasury Targets Networks Linked to Iran," August 29, 2014; (http://www.treasury.gov/press-center/press-releases/Pages/jl2618.aspx) & U.S. Department of State, Press Release, "Additional Sanctions Imposed by the Department of State Targeting Iranian Proliferators," August 29, 2014. (http://www.state.gov/r/pa/prs/ps/2014/231159.htm)

[56] Emanuele Ottolenghi & Saeed Ghasseminejad, "If The US Wants A Nuclear Deal, It Needs To Fully Enforce Its Sanctions Against Iran's Revolutionary Guards," *Business Insider*, September 19, 2014. (http://www.businessinsider.com/sanctioning-the-irgc-is-the-path-to-a-nuclear-deal-2014-9)

legislation. The main target of these sanctions is Iran's IRGC, including its overseas terrorist arm, the Quds Force, designated by the United States for terrorism since 2007.[57]

Congress should work with the Obama administration to enhance terrorism sanctions if Iran's terror finance and support for international terrorism continues, something the administration, as previously noted, has stated it is committed to doing. As government reports confirm, there remains strong evidence that Iran-backed terrorism has continued.[58]

At the same time, Iran's human rights record has, by numerous expert accounts, not improved under President Hassan Rouhani.[59] The United Nations Special Rapporteur on the Situation of Human Rights in the Islamic Republic of Iran concluded that human rights violations "persist, and in some cases appear to have worsened" over the past year.[60] Therefore, sanctions against Iranian human rights violators should remain in place regardless of a possible nuclear agreement with Iran.

Congress should work with the Obama administration to significantly expand U.S. human rights sanctions against any and all Iranian officials, entities, or instrumentalities engaged in human rights abuses. These designations would include targeted sanctions imposing travel bans and asset freezes on human rights abusers, economic sanctions against elements of the Iranian economy under their control, and stiff penalties against those who provide support to these abusers. A suggested list of potential sanctions targets includes the following Iranian persons and entities as well as any other persons or entities conducting transactions for or on behalf of these individuals or entities:

- the Supreme Leader of Iran;

- the President of Iran;

- a current or former key official of, manager or director of an entity that may be owned or controlled by, or senior adviser to:

    o the Supreme Leader of Iran;

    o the Office of the Supreme Leader of Iran;

    o the President of Iran;

    o the Office of the President of Iran;

---

[57] U.S. Department of State, Press Release, "Fact Sheet: Designation of Iranian Entities and Individuals for Proliferation Activities and Support for Terrorism," October 25, 2007. (http://2001-2009.state.gov/r/pa/prs/ps/2007/oct/94193.htm)

[58] U.S. Department of State, "State Sponsors of Terrorism Overview," *Country Reports on Terrorism 2013*, April 30, 2014. (http://www.state.gov/j/ct/rls/crt/2013/224826.htm)

[59] "Iranian Nobel Laureate: Human Rights As Bad As Under Ahmadinejad," *Associated Press*, November 12, 2014; (http://english.alarabiya.net/en/perspective/features/2014/11/12/Iranian-Nobel-laureate-Human-rights-as-bad-as-under-Ahmadinejad.html) & Sangwon Yoon, "Iran Leader Fails to Deliver on Rights Promises, UN Says," *Bloomberg*, October 27, 2014. (http://www.bloomberg.com/news/2014-10-27/iran-leader-fails-to-deliver-on-rights-promises-un-says.html)

[60] United Nations General Assembly, "Situation of Human Rights in the Islamic Republic of Iran," August 27, 2014, page 3. (http://shaheedoniran.org/wp-content/uploads/2014/09/A-69-356-SR-Report-Iran.pdf)

Congress designed many of the toughest sanctions that forced Tehran to the negotiation table. It should now therefore assert and act on its prerogative – and responsibility to its constituents – in helping to defend the core sanctions architecture it built.

Regardless of the post-November 24 scenario – whether the P5+1 and Iran reach a comprehensive agreement, reach a parameters agreement or expanded JPOA with an extension of the negotiations, or break off talks – Congress has a vital role to play to protect and enhance U.S. economic leverage. This leverage will be essential to enforce any deal and pressure Tehran to end the full range of its illicit activities. The worse the nuclear agreement – that is, the greater the amount of nuclear activity that Iran is allowed to maintain and the weaker the inspection, verification, and monitoring regime – the more important this economic leverage will become.

Unless the United States and our international partners are prepared to use military force to address every breach and every instance of non-compliance, American sanctions will be an effective mechanism to enforce any agreement and punish Iranian cheating so that the world is not threatened by a nuclear-armed Iran. Congress's role here can make the difference between a nuclear-armed Iran and an ensuing regional nuclear arms race and a more secure and stable region.

Thank you again for inviting me to testify before this distinguished Subcommittee. I look forward to your questions.

Congress designed many of the toughest sanctions that forced Tehran to the negotiation table. It should now therefore assert and act on its prerogative – and responsibility to its constituents – in helping to defend the core sanctions architecture it built.

Regardless of the post-November 24 scenario – whether the P5+1 and Iran reach a comprehensive agreement, reach a parameters agreement or expanded JPOA with an extension of the negotiations, or break off talks – Congress has a vital role to play to protect and enhance U.S. economic leverage. This leverage will be essential to enforce any deal and pressure Tehran to end the full range of its illicit activities. The worse the nuclear agreement – that is, the greater the amount of nuclear activity that Iran is allowed to maintain and the weaker the inspection, verification, and monitoring regime – the more important this economic leverage will become.

Unless the United States and our international partners are prepared to use military force to address every breach and every instance of non-compliance, American sanctions will be an effective mechanism to enforce any agreement and punish Iranian cheating so that the world is not threatened by a nuclear-armed Iran. Congress's role here can make the difference between a nuclear-armed Iran and an ensuing regional nuclear arms race and a more secure and stable region.

Thank you again for inviting me to testify before this distinguished Subcommittee. I look forward to your questions.

———

Ms. ROS-LEHTINEN. Mr. Sadjadpour.

STATEMENT OF MR. KARIM SADJADPOUR, SENIOR ASSOCIATE, MIDDLE EAST PROGRAM, CARNEGIE ENDOWMENT FOR INTERNATIONAL PEACE

Mr. SADJADPOUR. Thank you to the committee. It is a real honor to be here.

I would like to preface my comments by saying that I think everyone in this room shares the same goal. We want to avert a nuclear armed Iran. We want to avert another military conflict in the Middle East, and we want to see Iran's transformation into a more democratic, tolerant government.

I would like to focus my comments in three separate parts. First, internal implications of the nuclear talks within Iran, second the regional implications of the nuclear discussions and, third, the implications for U.S. policy.

Let me start with Iran internally. The paradox of Iran is the fact that you have a society which aspires to be like South Korea, prosperous and integrated, and you have a regime which shows a much greater resemblance to North Korea, prioritizing isolation, ideological purity, and militarization.

The optimists, proponents of a nuclear deal would argue that a deal could strengthen the hand of the moderates in Tehran and strengthen civil society. And, again, a more integrated Iran is good for the interests of our more pragmatic factions in Tehran.

Skeptics would argue the opposite that what we have seen in the last few weeks, as Representative Deutch alluded to, are increased human rights abuses. In the event of a deal, it is possible that the repressive apparatus of the Islamic republic will show even greater repression in order to signal to the population that external flexibility doesn't signal internal weakness.

My own take is that both of these outcomes are possible in the event of a deal. And that both Iranian civil society could be strengthened, but we will also see a backlash at the hand—by the Iranian hardliners. But it is important to note that Iranian—Iran civil society and human rights community has been overwhelmingly supportive of seeing a deal, whereas the more hardline, revolutionary elite in Tehran have expressed a real concern that this could possibly undermine their hold on power.

Let me move next to the regional implications of these regional talks. The optimists would argue that a nuclear deal could strengthen greater—could foster greater U.S.–U.N. cooperation in the Middle East on issues of mutual concern, whether that is Syria, Iraq, or Persian Gulf security. The skeptics would argue that a nuclear deal would actually provide Iran a financial boost to buttress forces like the Assad regime in Syria or to militant forces, whether in Hezbollah or Shiite militias in Iraq.

My own sense is that, over the last 35 years, we have seen tremendous consistency in Iran's foreign policy in the Middle East. I would argue the twin pillars of Iran's regional policy has been rejecting U.S. influence and rejecting Israel's existence. And I haven't seen, either a historic precedence or any recent evidence, to suggest that Iran is prepared to abandon these long-held principles in the region.

In fact, one of the fault lines between the moderate forces and Tehran and the hardliners is that moderate forces have, in the past, shown themselves willing to work with the United States against mutual regional adversaries, such as the Taliban, whereas hardline forces in Tehran have shown themselves willing to work with groups like Taliban or even al-Qaeda against the United States.

So my sense on the regional implications of these nuclear talks is that, as long as Iran's supreme leader, Ayatollah Khamenei, remains in power, we won't see any major changes in Iran's regional policies.

Let me end on talking about the implication for U.S. policy. I think, as one of the members alluded to earlier—and I would agree—my sense is that we will neither see a comprehensive resolution, nor a comprehensive failure come next Monday. We will more likely see a limited agreement used to justify an extension of the negotiations. I understand that, in the past, sanctions have proven to be effective at forcing Iran to come to the negotiating table and negotiate in a serious way.

My concern, however, is that in the event of an impasse, premature and unilateral sanctions by the United States, which don't enjoy the support of our allies, could actually jeopardize P5+1 unity and trigger Iran to reconstitute their program. I believe that Iran's abrogation of the interim deal should trigger additional sanctions, rather than additional sanctions triggering Iran's abrogation of the interim deal.

And lastly, I would just like to say that I believe that U.S. policies that have proven necessary to counter Iran's nuclear ambitions in a way are at loggerheads with U.S. policies necessary to facilitate Iran's—the transformation of political change within Iran. I believe that what we have seen necessary to counter Iran's nuclear ambitions has been economic and political isolation, whereas Iranian civil society, Iran's human rights community overwhelmingly believes that, in order to foster change in Iran, they need more political and economic intervention. So I think we need to think more creatively about how to reconcile these two policies. I will stop there.

Ms. ROS-LEHTINEN. Thank you very much.

[The prepared statement of Mr. Sadjadpour follows:]

CARNEGIE
ENDOWMENT FOR
INTERNATIONAL PEACE

Congressional Testimony

House Foreign Affairs Subcommittee on the
Middle East and Northern Africa

"Examining What a Nuclear Iran Deal Means for
Global Security"

Testimony by **Karim Sadjadpour**
Senior Associate, Middle East Program
Carnegie Endowment for International Peace

November 20, 2014

The Paradox of Iran

The paradox of Iran is that of a society which aspires to be like South Korea—prosperous and globally-integrated—hindered by a hardline revolutionary elite whose ideological rigidity and isolationism more closely resembles North Korea. During Iran's 2013 presidential campaign Hassan Rouhani marketed himself to both these interest groups as the man who could reconcile the ideological prerogatives of the Islamic Republic with the economic interests of the Iranian nation. Despite these raised expectations, however, Iran today remains a country of enormous but unfulfilled potential.

From the outset of his presidency, Rouhani understood that Iran's economic malaise could not be reversed without lifting sanctions, and lifting sanctions requires a nuclear deal. He accordingly invested all of his political capital in nuclear diplomacy rather than domestic affairs, and refrained from unsettling Iran's conservatives—whose support he needs to secure a nuclear compromise—with talk of democracy and human rights, or an alteration of Tehran's regional policies. The combination of an interim nuclear deal, normalized U.S-Iran dialogue, and the appointment of competent economic managers has helped curb rampant inflation, increase oil exports, and improve private sector confidence.

While Iran's economic has shown modest signs of improvement, however, Iranian civil society who supported Rouhani contend that more than a year later, little has changed. According to Ahmad Shaheed, the United Nations Special Rapporteur on the situation of human rights in Iran, since Rouhani's elections Iran's already high execution rate has increased substantially, and the persecution of religious minorities remains widespread. In recent weeks the Islamic Republic of Iran reminded the world it is a place where young women risk acid attacks for "bad hejab", imprisonment for attending male volleyball matches, and execution for protecting themselves against alleged rapists.

While Rouhani's international detractors accuse him of being duplicitous, his domestic supporters worry that the fate of his presidency rests largely on a nuclear deal that he does not have the authority to complete. Critical decisions such as the nuclear file continue to require the blessing of Supreme Leader Ayatollah Ali Khamenei together with the Islamic Revolutionary Guard Corps, whose political and economic interests appear to be symbiotic. While a clear majority of Iran's population and much of the outside world want to see Iran emerge from political and economic isolation, the Islamic Republic's 35-year history has shown us that what hardliners lack in popular support, they make up for in coercive strength.

Implications of a nuclear deal for Iran internally

Optimists hope that a nuclear deal will empower Tehran's moderate officials and embolden civil society, creating a more tolerant, auspicious environment for reform. Skeptics fear that in the aftermath of any deal the Islamic Republic will heighten its repressive apparatus to show its public that external flexibility doesn't signal internal weakness. These scenarios are not mutually exclusive, in that a nuclear deal could both embolden moderates and invite a backlash from hardliners.

What's important to note is that Iranian civil society has expressed near universal support for a nuclear accommodation. While not all are hopeful that it will lead to greater civil liberties, they believe a more internationally integrated Iran is conducive to the advancement of an open society. Contemporary history corroborates their instincts. In the Islamic Republic's 35-years the country's most repressive periods have been at times of external conflict and crises, which Tehran's hardliners have often instigated, exploited, and prolonged for internal political expediency, such as the 1979 hostage crisis.

Indeed, for Iran's hardliners the economic welfare of its citizens has always been secondary to domestic political expediency and revolutionary ideology. They shrewdly understand their authority is best preserved in isolation--similar to their allies in places like Pyongyang and Havana--and enmity with the United States is needed for internal legitimation. A nuclear deal that reduces Iran's isolation, potentially strengthens moderates at home, and raises popular expectations for further rapprochement with the U.S. could be more threatening to regime stability than a continued standoff.

Implications of a nuclear deal for Iran's foreign policy

Advocates of a nuclear deal often assert that it would strengthen Tehran's moderates and auger greater U.S.-Iran regional cooperation on contentious matters such as Syria, Iraq, and Persian Gulf security. Skeptics fear a deal would not only fail to moderate Iran's regional policies, but would also provide Tehran a significant financial boost to buttress the Assad regime in Damascus and other regional proxies hostile to the U.S. and Israel.

While domestic Iranian politics is famously unpredictable, there is no historic precedent nor recent evidence to suggest the Islamic Republic might abandon or modify its longstanding revolutionary principles, namely opposition to U.S. influence and Israel's existence. Throughout the last three decades these pillars of Iran's foreign policy have shown little signs of change, despite the election of moderate presidents or tremendous financial strain due to sanctions and/or low oil prices.

This is despite the fact that since 1979 the U.S. and Iran have faced common adversaries in the USSR, Saddam Hussein, the Taliban, al-Qaeda, and now ISIS. Indeed, as Henry Kissinger once wrote, "there are few nations in the world with whom the U.S. has more common interests and less reason to quarrel than Iran." Yet successive U.S. presidents tried and failed to turn these overlapping interests into a cooperative working relationship.

While the overlap in U.S. and Iranian interests may at times allow for tactical cooperation, as long as Ayatollah Khamenei remains Supreme Leader Iran is likely to maintain strategic enmity with the United States. One of the fault lines between Iran's so-called "principlists"—those who believe in fealty to the principles of the 1979 revolution—and its pragmatists is the fact that the latter have been willing to work with the United States against Sunni radical groups (such as the Taliban and al-Qaeda), while the former have been willing to work with Sunni radical groups against the United States.

Though Khamenei's hostility is cloaked in ideology, in reality it's driven by self-preservation. As the powerful cleric Ahmad Jannati once noted, "If pro-American tendencies come to power in Iran, we have to say goodbye to everything. After all, anti-Americanism is among the main features of our Islamic state." More recently in July 2014 Khamenei himself asserted that

"Reconciliation between Iran and America is possible…but reconciliation between the Islamic Republic and Iran is not."

Managing irresolution

There is a strong possibility that nuclear negotiations will result in neither a comprehensive resolution nor a comprehensive failure, but a limited agreement and extended negotiations. In such a scenario the role of Congress remains especially critical. While the precise merits and demerits of a limited deal and the terms of an extension cannot be assessed beforehand, two broad principals are important to keep in mind:

- Any scenario must be measured against not a utopian ideal (the total dismantlement of Iran's nuclear program), but realistic alternatives.
- The intent of U.S. policy should be to deter Iran's nuclear advancement, not provoke it.

Given the wide-spread assessment of the United States and European allies that economic pressure forced Tehran to seriously negotiate, Congress might be tempted to enact additional sanctions in order to coerce an Iranian compromise. Premature, unilateral U.S. sanctions, however, run the risk of jeopardizing P5+1 unity, tainting America's favorable standing among the Iranian people, and precipitating a conflict.

Rather the force greater Iranian nuclear concessions, additional sanctions would more likely encourage Iran to recommence its nuclear activities and curtail its already limited cooperation with the International Atomic Energy Association (IAEA). Iran's calculations—which may prove to be miscalculations—are in part driven by the view that President Obama is desperate for a foreign policy victory and Washington, not Tehran, will be blamed for abrogating the collectively agreed upon Joint Plan of Action (JPOA).

While the global embargo of the Iranian economy has up until now remained largely intact, in the event of a diplomatic breakdown it's uncertain whether Europe, Russia, and Asia will continue to forsake their own commercial and strategic ties with Iran to placate the United States. In contrast to the era of bombastic Iranian president Mahmoud Ahmadinejad, today China, Russia, and even many European allies believe Iran is too critical to Middle East stability to be shunned, and President Rouhani and Foreign Minister Zarif are reasonable leaders who should be engaged and strengthened, not sanctioned and weakened.

The worst scenario for U.S. interests is one in which Congress overwhelmingly passes new sanctions, Iran resumes its nuclear activities, and international unity unravels. Such an outcome would force the United States to revisit the possibility of another military conflict in the Middle East, an option that few Americans favor.

In this context, Congressional legislation should be devised to lock-in Iran's current compromises, deter Iranian encroachment, and incentivize greater Iranian compromises. In essence, Iran should have both strong disincentives to move forward together with strong incentives to compromise. In order to maintain international unity it's important that Iranian encroachment trigger additional Congressional sanctions, rather than Congressional sanctions triggering Iranian encroachment. Put another way, congressional sanctions should be conceived in order to deter Iran's nuclear ambitions, not provoke them.

It's also important for Congress to think more creatively about ways to align itself with the aspirations of the Iranian people, not only against the nuclear aspirations of the Iranian government. U.S. policies necessary to counter Iran's nuclear program and the policies needed to facilitate political transformation in Iran are at loggerheads. The economic pressure and political isolation that have proven necessary to force Tehran to reassess its nuclear ambitions are hurtful to Iranian civil society and the private sector, which require political and economic engagement.

Ms. Ros-Lehtinen. Thank you to all of our witnesses. I will begin the question-and-answer period.

As the author of the strongest set of sanctions currently on the books, the Iran Threat Reduction and Syria Human Rights Act of 2012 and the Iran Freedom Support Act of 2006, I know how hard it was to have these sanctions with teeth and how hard it is to get the administration to enforce them.

The P5+1 started from a position of weakness and proceeded to give up too much too fast, and the Iranians have taken advantage every step of the way. The Iranians cannot be trusted. It is impossible to verify their nuclear program, and Rouhani has been on record bragging about his ability to deceive the administration.

General Hayden, you have said that Iran and its nuclear program are among the things that keep you awake at night. You are also on record as saying that Iran isn't coming clean about its past weaponization activities or submitting to snap inspections of suspect facilities and that if you were still the Director of the CIA, you would ''advise the President that the agreement could not be adequately verified.''

The IAEA has said that Iran is not in compliance and can't verify its nuclear program, and our intel community has assessed that we cannot independently verify Iran's nuclear program.

Therefore, General Hayden, I will ask you this: What kind of threat is posed to the interests of the United States, to our allies, to global security since the administration is constructing a deal that can't be verified or monitored? And what could be the impact if Iran were to actually secure a nuclear weapon?

Secondly, how will the other actors in the region respond to a deal that can't be trusted? And, lastly, given the fact that our intelligence has not been able to detect Iran's nefarious activities in the past, how can we believe that we can detect them now?

General Hayden. Thank you, ma'am.

First of all, just point of clarification: We can't verify this agreement in a noncooperative regime. All right. That is why we need the robust inspection regime.

So I was asked this question as I was leaving government during the transition. So how many nuclear—well, what is Iranian nuclear doctrine? And I answered quite honestly, ''I have no idea.'' And, well, how many weapons do you think they will get? Oh, three, four, I am not sure. How many do we have? Oh, tens of thousands. So, then, why can't we deter them? And I said, ''Ah, now we have come to—now we have come to the matter.'' This is not about deterring them. This is about deterring us.

Look at Iranian behavior without one of these kits in the garage. And I use those terms carefully. Even without the test, even without the nuclear detonation, a parking close enough to the nuclear weapons reality that there is great ambiguity, how much more confidence do we give the Islamic republic in continuing the kinds of activities that we have seen them do and you have cataloged in your commentary at the beginning of the hour? How much more involvement in Iraq and Syria and Afghanistan, in the Gulf do we see when they have got one of these things, which is kind of that whole card that they can turn face up at any time?

With regard to what the neighborhood does, the definitive fault line now in this part of the world isn't Arab-Israeli, isn't moderate, religious, secular—the defining fault line here is Sunni-Shiia. And that may be good, it may be bad. But it certainly is.

I can't conceive of the Sunni states continuing to exist with a Shiia state, Iran, having or too close to having a nuclear weapon without taking actions on their own. And so here I would see nuclear development within these countries, perhaps not going to creating fissile materials.

But let me give you a thought, a scenario that surely can't bring you much comfort. How about a Pakistani nuclear guarantee for the Kingdom of Saudi Arabia in the face of Iranian nuclear weapons programs? Now, that can't make you sleep well at night?

Ms. ROS-LEHTINEN. Thank you very much. Thank you.

Thank you, gentlemen.

I would now turn to Mr. Deutch of Florida.

Mr. DEUTCH. Thank you.

Thanks, Madam Chairman.

I wanted to just ask you about what a lot of us take as a threshold issue here, which is how can we expect to reach any sort of comprehensive agreement that is verifiable if we don't—if we are not able to get past the very fundamental questions of the history of Iran's nuclear program?

In 2020—it is now more than 2 years ago that the P5+1 asked that the IAEA be able to finish its work in Parchin. And, to date, at least as far as I know, the Iranians haven't permitted that. If they can't come clean about the past military dimensions of the program, how is it possible to expect that any agreement can be valid going forward?

Mr. DUBOWITZ. Well, Congressman Deutch, I mean, you are exactly right. We can't have that confidence. And, again, I think this has been misrepresented in the public domain, that this is about Iran's mea culpa, that Iran has to come clean and make a confession. This is not about a confession.

This is about can you design—as you alluded to, can you design a proper verification and inspection regime? Because if you don't know where Iran was conducting its past weaponization activities—and, by the way, the IAEA says that there are still possible military dimensions of the program still ongoing. Then, if you can't—if you don't know where they did it, if you can't interview the people involved, if you can't see the documentation, if you don't have eyes into those details, then, it is very difficult to design a comprehensive verification and inspection regime for the future.

And so, this is why PMDs are so critical. This is why the French, for example, have made PMDs their key issue. And without that comprehensive verification and inspection regime, that is, as General Hayden said, go anywhere, go any time, snap inspections, we can see IRGC bases, we can go into military bases, any suspected establishment we have access to, then, we have no ability to detect an Iranian breakout, sneak-out or fake-out. And that has been the history of Iranian nuclear mendacity for 30 years.

Mr. DEUTCH. General Hayden, we always—we tend to get caught up in the discussion of the moment and now PMD is just part of this overall discussion.

But in your experience, what is the real concern that—that the whole discussion of the military dimension of the program, what we know, what we don't know? What is the real concern and how should that impact our discussions going forward?

General HAYDEN. Congressman, the real concern is we don't know the point at which they are now parked, in terms. And, here, we are really talking about the weaponization program. We are really talking about the hardening, the miniaturization, the science that is involved in creating the nuclear detonation. That is not the long pole on the tent.

The long pole on the tent is the fissile material. And if you recall, even in 2007, when we said "good evidence they have stopped weaponization," they kept working on the long pole, which was the fissile materials. And so you have got fissile material being developed—sorry, Congressman. Let me—let me give a slightly longer——

Mr. DEUTCH. Sure.

General HAYDEN [continuing]. Answer because something strikes me.

In the transition, again, to the Obama administration, we had an NSC meeting about Iran. And the President asked me, "How many kilos of LEU and medium-enriched uranium do they have?" And I said, "Mr. President, I actually know the answer to that and I am going to give it to you in a minute, but let me give you another way of thinking about this."

There isn't a neutron or an electron in Natanz that is ever going to show up in a nuclear weapon. Okay. What they are building out in Natanz is confidence. What they are building out in Natanz is technology and the ability to do this. They are going to build the fissile material for a weapon, the HEU, at a site about which we have no knowledge. Okay.

And so this—as Mark points out, our lack of knowledge, our lack of an ability to go to locations where they may be doing these things gives me very little confidence that we know how—as I said, we are not going to get an agreement that absolutely prevents. We are going to get an agreement that creates enough space for us to do something between the decision to go and the decision to have.

Mr. DEUTCH. Thank you, General Hayden.

Mr. Sadjadpour, in my remaining few seconds: Does the Iranian—do the Iranian people want the right to enrich as much or more than a government that is not repressive, that doesn't violate human rights, that respects freedom of the press and so on?

Mr. SADJADPOUR. Representative Deutch, there has never been an open discussion in Iran about the nuclear issue.

Recently, a prominent intellectual, Sadegh Zibakalam, who questioned the wisdom of Iran's nuclear program was sentenced to 18 months in prison. So, despite the fact that the government says that the population is united behind the program, they don't allow for open debate.

Recently, a former minister in Iran said the ancillary costs of the nuclear program have been upwards of $400 billion. I think if you posed the referendum to the Iranian people, "Would you like $400 billion to be spent on hospitals and schools, or would you like $400 billion spent on an antiquate nuclear program, which has isolated the country politically and economically,'' I think the vast majority would prefer the former. But this is a program, which is not driven by the Iranian people, but by the Iranian Government.

Ms. Ros-Lehtinen. Thank you so much.

Mr. Wilson of South Carolina.

Mr. Wilson. Thank you, Madam Chairman. And thank you for your leadership on this issue.

And we appreciate each one of you being here today. And, Mr. Sadjadpour, your analogy of Korea was very thought provoking, and I really hope the people of Iran think about it, too, because the extraordinary success of South Korea is something to be emulated everywhere in the world. And it was really intriguing.

General Hayden, in your testimony, you mentioned creative solutions and what—that we should be cautious of them. Could you expand on what a creative solution is and why we should be wary?

General Hayden. The one I had in mind, Congressman, was the one that have been floated with regard to the number of centrifuges. I know what all of us in the room would like, is that the right number is zero. But I think the cost of admission to the current negotiations was an agreement that there would be some enrichment in Iran. Now, we can judge whether that is good or bad, but I think it truly is.

So, now, the debate is how many. All right. My very unscientific number is maybe four to 5,000. The regime has 19,000. The Supreme Leader is talking in tens and scores of thousands.

The creative solution we have is, well, they wouldn't dismantle the centrifuges. They disconnect the plumbing so you couldn't use them in sequence to enrich uranium. It is those kinds of things that make me uncomfortable. That the Iranians are holding their ground—just in the tactics of negotiations, they are holding their ground and we are coming up with, ''Well, how about this'' as another way to get some sort of an agreement. I am just made very uncomfortable about that.

Mr. Wilson. And thank you for your insight because it really is very important.

Mr. Dubowitz, in your testimony, you reference analysis of a recent IAEA report that indicates Iran has directly violated terms of the joint plan of action. How has the administration responded to this evidence of Iranian cheating? I am concern that Iran will continue in incremental cheating, and the international community won't respond effectively.

What kind of punishments for breaches to the JPOA or violations of a possible comprehensive agreement should be put in place to send a message that no cheating of any sort would be tolerated?

Mr. Dubowitz. Congressman, thank you for the question. And, actually, it gets to Karim's comment that, you know, we should set up it so that Iran's abrogation should trigger sanctions. Well, in fact, if H.R. 850 and S–1881 had been in place, those sanctions in waiting would have been triggered and rightfully so, because the Iranians were cheating on the JPOA. And what they were doing is they were introducing UF6 gas into an advanced centrifuge, into the IR5. And that was a violation of the JPOA. It was in the IA report, and it was detected and publicized by David Albright.

And this is an example of what Iran does when I say "they cheat incrementally and not egregiously" and that they are testing the boundaries of our willingness to respond. And there was no response. There were no sanctions. There was no economic cost. And the message to Iran is, when there is a comprehensive agreement, you can cheat incrementally, you can exploit ambiguities, you can find workarounds. And the Iranians are experts at doing this. The regime is an expert sanctions buster. It is also an expert at busting the spirit and the commitments that they make.

And so what can we put in place? Well, what we have to put in place is significant economic leverage. We have to be able to hit them hard economically when they cheat. So when they don't let inspectors into Parchin number 1, 2, 3 and 5, when they start moving ahead on advanced centrifuge R&D, when they do a number of the things that they are going to do to cheat, we have to have sufficient economic leverage.

My fear and my testimony is that we are going to surrender that economic leverage, the President is going to suspend sanctions and, through that sanctions relief, Iran's economy is going to increase, it is going to harden, it is going to become more durable, and it is going to be much more difficult to then use economic leverage to force them back into compliance.

Mr. WILSON. And the response of the Obama administration was no response at all?

Mr. DUBOWITZ. Well, public reporting confirmed that the administration has heard what Mr. Albright had said and had spoken to the Iranians, and the Iranians denied having done it, and the administration assures us that the Iranians are not doing it anymore, so——

Mr. WILSON. Well, that would be no response. And I share your concern.

In regard to the financial based sanctions, have they been effective?

Mr. DUBOWITZ. Financial sanctions have been very effective. And I just want to point out, again, your letter of July 20th makes this very clear, those financial sanctions are not nuclear sanctions. Secretary Lew, Under Secretary Cohen, Under Secretary—former Under Secretary Levy have all made clear that the sanctions, the financial sanctions that have been put in place are because of a range of Iran's elicit activities. It is nuclear, it is ballistic missile, it is terrorism, it is money laundering, it is elicit financial conduct.

In fact, administration officials have repeatedly said we put the financial sanctions in place to protect the integrity of the global financial system. It would be a big mistake to unwind those financial sanctions because we have a nuclear deal. We have seen this movie before, it was called North Korea. And the unwinding of the sanctions against Banco Delta Asia, and we saw two subsequent nuclear tests after that and the unwinding of the tough financial sanctions against North Korea.

Mr. WILSON. Thank you very much.

Ms. ROS-LEHTINEN. Thank you, Mr. Wilson.

Mr. Higgins of New York.

Mr. HIGGINS. Thank you, Madam Chair.

General Hayden, you had said that the knowledge of the Iranian nuclear program is incomplete. And here is what we do know. The growth of the program, obviously, in the last decade has been explosive—163 centrifuges, which are the machines that I understand mix at supersonic speeds to enrich uranium to bomb-grade. There are now 19,000. There are heavy water reactors, which are used to create plutonium, which is another bomb fuel.

My concern is not as much even for the current capacity of Iran to create a nuclear weapon; it is the second and third generation. It is the things that they are doing now. It is the knowledge in this multibillion-dollar atomic infrastructure, or they created it, which is a huge part of the economy and finances the Revolutionary Guard, that you can't destroy knowledge.

So what is it additionally that we don't know? Because I will tell you something. From what we do know, it is pretty compelling that we shouldn't pull back on sanctions, that we should be accelerating.

You know, the Supreme Leader, Khamenei, used to say, you know, that the sanctions don't hurt us, you know, they make us stronger, they make us economically independent. But his statements in the last, you know, 12 months, he is talking about, you know, the sanctions are brutal, both in terms of inflation and oil output and currency valuation, even to the extent that you can't get chickens at Ramadan because there is no chicken feed.

So what don't we know?

General HAYDEN. Well, number one, Congressman, we don't know where everything is. All right? The facilities we know we know, and we don't know what we don't know.

Qom, for example, Fordow, all right? We discovered that before it became operational, but it was fairly far along before we discovered it. And it was a major facility, and we actually had some help in order to make our initial discovery there.

We don't know about the weaponization program, the details. How far along are they, for example? How quickly are they transforming from IR–1s to IR–2s, the advanced centrifuges?

So, to take your point, as they build competence, as they build technology, the footprint that they need to do the breakout sprint to highly enriched uranium, that footprint becomes smaller and smaller.

And back to my point, they are not going to do this at Natanz, because they have to kick the IAEA out, literally, to do that. That is a trigger. They are going to do it somewhere else, a somewhere else about which we have no knowledge at the present time. And this gets harder to detect as their efficiency increases and, again, the footprint that has to be shown gets smaller and smaller.

Mr. HIGGINS. Mr. Dubowitz, you said that Iran is at the table because of sanctions. And that is your area of expertise, the sanctions history.

What is it that we are not doing that we ought to be doing to further apply pressure on the Iranian regime?

Mr. DUBOWITZ. So, very specifically, Iran still exports 1.3 million barrels of oil——

Mr. HIGGINS. To?

Mr. DUBOWITZ [continuing]. And an additional couple hundred thousand barrels of condensates.

Mr. HIGGINS. To? To whom?

Mr. DUBOWITZ. They are exporting it to China, India, Japan, South Korea, Turkey, and Taiwan.

Mr. HIGGINS. Okay. Keep going.

Mr. DUBOWITZ. And H.R. 850, which has cleared your committee, would have taken a significant bite out of those exports. It would have closed the condensates loophole. It would have denied them essential oil revenues.

They also have $120 billion of oil revenues sitting in escrow accounts around the world. They are semi-restricted, meaning they can only spend that money in the six countries that I named earlier on bilateral trade. So you could——

Mr. HIGGINS. Where is that money being held?

Mr. DUBOWITZ. It is, again, held in China, India, Japan, South Korea, Turkey, and Taiwan——

Mr. HIGGINS. Yep.

Mr. DUBOWITZ [continuing]. And only used for bilateral trade purposes. But Iran can use the money. So you could lock up the full $120 billion and deny them all of that revenue and they wouldn't have money to fund their imports.

Again, those are two ideas that would take a serious bite out of the Iranian economy.

And, more importantly, it sometimes is not the substance of the sanctions, it is the psychology of sanctions. In an escalating sanctions environment, like we saw between 2007 and 2013, the psychological blow of sanctions created a sense of fear in international markets and a sense of despair in the Iranian domestic economy. And that translated into a severe economic recession that Iran is now emerging from.

Mr. HIGGINS. Okay.

My time has expired.

Mr. DESANTIS [presiding]. The gentleman's time has expired.

The Chair now recognizes the gentleman from Illinois for 5 minutes.

Mr. KINZINGER. Well, I thank the chairman.

And thank you all for being here.

And, General, it is great to see you. From one Air Force guy to another, I thank you for your service.

It is sad because, to me, you know, we are sitting around talking about what could happen or what will happen, and none of this surprises me. I mean, honestly, I could have told you a year ago that we would be extending the interim agreement for 6 months, that we wouldn't come to a conclusion, that we would be sitting here 4 days prior to the 1-year deadline and probably will get some kind of a request, either a terrible deal that miraculously has a breakthrough at the end or, more than likely, another request for an additional 6 months or however long the administration will want, which, to me, is going to be interesting because I don't understand what can happen in a further 6 months or any further time period that could compel Iran to come to the table that hasn't been able to occur in the first year. I mean, there is not going to be any additional step-up of pain or anything like that.

I also think it is important to remind everybody, especially when we talk about ISIS but when we talk about this issue too, Iran is not our friend. Probably a significant number of American casualties that occurred in the war I was in in Iraq occurred directly or indirectly from Iran—from Iranian actions directly, from Iranian technology that was exported to terrorists for one purpose, to kill American soldiers. That is why it was sent. So this technology was compiled in Iran and exported to Iraq for the sole purpose of killing young men and women from the United States of America. Okay? Let's just remember that. This is the Iran that we are talking about.

And now we find ourselves in a situation where, you know, we are 4 days out from trying to guarantee that they won't build a nuclear weapon. We have to send a message to South Korea that has begged for the right to do some kind of reprocessing and recycling that we are going to give, potentially, the right to enrich to our worst enemy but yet our best friend, among our best friends, will not have the equal right. We all know that debate.

I have a question that I would like to ask first off. Let's talk a little bit about what happened in North Korea. I was a young guy when there was the discussion of possibly striking locations in North Korea. I believe that President Clinton at one point had been ready to give the go order, and then it was backed off when a breakthrough deal was reached with North Korea to prevent them from obtaining nuclear weapons. We all know that basically, theoretically, a little bit later, they had a big parade and we saw nuclear weapons and they were nuclearized.

What lessons did we learn from that that we ought to apply to this moment here? I know you guys addressed North Korea when I was out of the room, so if we are reiterating, please forgive me. So I want to talk about that.

And the other thing I want to say is this—or the other question I want to ask is this. What kind of a message is it going to send, not just to Iran but to Russia, to all these hotspots we are dealing with around the world, if at the point the deadline, the red line comes up with a deal with Iran we simply extend it and go back to negotiations?

So, General, I will start with you, both the issue of North Korea as well as the issue of what message are we going to send to the world and not just in the Iran situation.

General HAYDEN. Thanks, Congressman. I will be very efficient.

When we were negotiating with the North Koreans in 2008, early 2009, I mean, our judgment was simply they are not going to give up their weapons program. They can't. It would be irrational on their part, given their world view. All right? There is a bit of that inside the Iranian regime, as well. And, you know, my job is to try to think like they think, so forgive me while I lay out the point of view from a serious person in Tehran.

They went to school on what happened to Muammar Qadhafi. All right? Here was someone who gave up his WMD program in negotiations with the United States in return for what he perceived to be a bit more welcoming international community. And we ended up over a 10-month period with a sustained bombing campaign under NATO, overthrowing that government and leading to his death.

And so even the calmer people in Tehran, you know, not the apocalyptic ones, are saying, oh, so that is what happens to you when you give up this kind of program. So I don't have to demonize the Iranians to tell you I have come to the conclusion that this is too important to them for them to give it up.

When we went out of the gate the first time—what now, 10 months ago?—I was very careful with my public commentary to be broadly supportive of the negotiations. I wanted to exhaust all possibilities. But I learned in my last job at CIA to think ahead, think of what you think—think of what people are going to want you to think in 10 months. And so I thought through the process of, what if we don't get an agreement in 6? What is an okay process then?

And when we began—I am talking 10 or 11 months ago—my conclusion was, I will give it one more 6, I will give it one more period. But what we can't stand is the diplomatic equivalent of a continuing resolution, you know, where we have them too close and we are not pushing them back.

Mr. KINZINGER. Thank you.

I would love to hear from you, but we are out of time, so I will I yield back.

Thanks.

Ms. ROS-LEHTINEN [presiding]. Thank you, sir.

Mr. Cicilline of Rhode Island.

Mr. CICILLINE. Thank you, Madam Chair.

And thank you to the witnesses.

General Hayden, I want to build on what you were just saying. So if it is, in fact, the case that the Iranians or the regime believe that the development of a nuclear weapons program is necessary for their self-defense, is there any reason to have any hope that there will ever be a resolution which includes an agreement to dismantle the program that they find necessary for their self-defense? Or is there some other set of systems or defense capability that would replace, potentially, their belief that they need it to defend themselves? Or is that just beyond——

General HAYDEN. I don't think there is a military answer from their point of view that gives them the same kind of assurance that the ambiguity of the program, not the actual detonation, maybe not even the possession—that is why good people—number one, Congressman, that is why this is a problem from hell. There are no good off ramps.

But that is also why some good people, like Amos Yadlin, who was my counterpart in the Israeli Defense Force—General Yadlin thinks you can't get the small deal, ''small'' as being defined as the nuclear deal. You can only get the nuclear deal inside of a much larger deal between Iran and the West. And we have already talked about how difficult that would be, given all of the other parameters.

Mr. CICILLINE. So you take that assessment and you add to it the testimony you provided with respect to the incredible difficulty, maybe impossibility, of verifying the activities of the regime. When you take those two facts together, does it make it even less likely?

General HAYDEN. Yes, sir, it does.

Look, when I do this publicly, I do a little Venn diagram in the ether here. Here is everything the Iranians can legitimately give up. Here is everything we legitimately need.

Mr. CICILLINE. They don't intersect.

General HAYDEN. They don't intersect.

Mr. CICILLINE. So, then, if, in fact, the conclusion of these negotiations is some determination that we can't reach an agreement and the parties stop the negotiations, I would like to know what your assessment is of what happens next.

Mr. Dubowitz, Mr. Sadjadpour might also add to it, but starting with General Hayden.

General HAYDEN. That is why we left this an ugly baby for the next administration. We didn't have any good answers.

You know, the other answer is, well, then, we have to go physical, we have to go kinetic. And Secretary Gates used to consistently say in our meetings, if we go kinetic, we will guarantee that which we are trying to prevent, an Iran that will stop at nothing, in secret, to develop a nuclear weapon.

Mr. CICILLINE. And do you think that is——

General HAYDEN. Yeah. Yes, sir.

Mr. CICILLINE. Mr. Dubowitz?

Mr. DUBOWITZ. So, Congressman, I think there is, first of all, another kinetic option and there is another economic option.

The kinetic option is not necessarily to strike Iran's nuclear facilities today. The kinetic option is to actually ground the Assad air force, an air force that is dropping barrel bombs on Syrian men, women, and children. The Syrian regime is Iran's closest ally in the Middle East. They have gone all-in to support Assad.

And it is also going to be critically important to the defeat of ISIL that we actually are finding a way to support the Syrian Sunnis, who have been increasingly radicalized because of the butchery of the Assad regime, and they have turned, as a result, to ISIL.

So I think the kinetic option is to actually—as part of the administration's Syria review process is to look at grounding Assad's air force and moving militarily against Iran's closest ally in the Middle East.

The economic option is—again, there are a tidal wave of sanctions that are possible. There are also phased, calibrated sanctions that will begin to tighten the squeeze on Iran and do so in a way that is not going to necessarily lead to a significant nuclear physics escalation from the Iranians.

Mr. CICILLINE. But can I ask you, Mr. Dubowitz, on the—with respect to additional sanctions, you know, I have read a lot of material that talks about the ability of the leadership of the regime to sort of protect themselves from the impact of sanctions and, in fact, to even benefit from some of the market conditions that result from sanctions.

And it seems to me, long-term sanctions can only work if ultimately they create conditions which cause people in the country to assert pressure on the government or the regime to change. And it doesn't sound like, from any of the testimony today or anything we have heard in this committee, that there is any likelihood that that pressure is going to be sufficiently strong to actually change the regime so long as things like the gentleman who spoke out and is imprisoned for 18 months for just questioning the worthiness of the program.

So, you know, speak to that question of, how do we impact, you know, the folks who are making the decisions in the regime, who I think sometimes actually benefit from these sanctions?

Mr. DUBOWITZ. So the elites will always benefit, but the question is, can you shake the economy—the macroeconomic fundamentals of an economy, that the regime fears economic collapse?

And what we saw in 2009, combined with 2012 and 2013, was millions of people on the street in 2009, yelling, "Death to the dictator," "President Obama, are you with us or with the dictator?," and in 2011, 2012, an economy that was facing a balance-of-payments crisis and that was in a severe recession, which combined to create fear in the regime that this Green Revolution would become a blue revolution, that it would lead to millions and tens of millions of Iranians outside of the middle-class suburbs of North Tehran but into the cities and towns of Iran and labor strikes in the key energy sector—in fact, conditions that we saw in 1979 that led to the Iranian revolution in the first place.

That combination created terror, in my view, and the regime has avoided that now. They have repressed the Green movement, as Karim has said, and they have also dealt with this economic stress by moving away from a severe recession into a modest economic recovery, thanks to the sanctions relief and the de-escalation of sanctions pressure.

Mr. CICILLINE. Thank you.

I yield back.

Ms. ROS-LEHTINEN. Thank you, sir.

Dr. Yoho?

Mr. YOHO. Thank you, Madam Chair.

I appreciate you guys being here today.

And, General, if you had a hard time sleeping before, I am sure you have a really hard time sleeping now. I never have a hard time sleeping, but I do now since I have been on Foreign Affairs.

I have been here for 2 years—this is my first term—and I have had multiple hearings on this subject. All the experts have said that Iran is, you know, 5, 6 months away from having enough material to have a nuclear bomb. That was 1 year ago, so I can only assume they have enough material.

And I agree with you in that their two pillars are the rejection of U.S. influence and the rejection of Israel's existence. I don't think they have wavered on that. And I have watched this for over 30 years, since the oil embargoes of the 1970s.

And they are hellbent on getting a nuclear weapon. Would you agree with that?

General HAYDEN. I would change that slightly. They want to keep that door open, and visibly open, that they have the nuclear option to exercise, to go to a weapon.

Mr. YOHO. Okay. But what I am seeing for the last 30 years is a cat-and-mouse game where they say they are not doing it but we find out they are, and they are doing it——

General HAYDEN. Oh, they are clearly—they are clearly setting the stage for it.

Mr. YOHO. And so we know what their intent is.

And I guess a couple questions I have here: How do you get Iran to roll back their program? What is the impetus that is going to make them roll back?

Because with the sanctions that have been in place, they were still continuing. They have not stopped. They have gotten closer, and they have got the ICBM program going on. And I agree 100 percent with you; what they are doing is refining the technology. They don't need as many centrifuges. They are more efficient with the smaller ones or the higher-tech ones. So they can do a better job, and they can keep that hidden, covert.

In order to negotiate an agreement, there has to be trust, understanding, character, integrity, and verification. I have seen none of that. I mean, they throw the IAEA out, the International Atomic Energy Agency out every chance they get, or they prevent them from going in. We know they have exploded a nuclear trigger device, but they have covered that up. They have covered it up with a parking lot. And there is just no trust there.

And so, with these negotiations, do you feel the sanctions were backed off too early?

General HAYDEN. That is a tough call.

Mr. YOHO. Mr. Dubowitz, how about you?

Mr. DUBOWITZ. I am certainly on record repeatedly saying that. I mean, I think that we had brought them very close to a——

Mr. YOHO. I agree.

Mr. DUBOWITZ [continuing]. Balance-of-payments crisis, and 4 or 5 more months of sanctions escalation would have presented this regime—and let me just actually—it is not just me saying this.

Mr. YOHO. No.

Mr. DUBOWITZ. When Rouhani came into office, he said it.

Mr. YOHO. Right.

Mr. DUBOWITZ. I mean, he actually came out and said, ''It is worse than I expected.'' Now, politicians always say that. ''The other guy did a bad job'' and——

Mr. YOHO. Right.

Mr. DUBOWITZ [continuing]. Lowering expectations so that I can exceed them. But you had many Iranian officials—the President, economic officials—coming out and saying, ''This economy is a complete mess. It is worse than we expected.''

Mr. YOHO. Right.

Mr. DUBOWITZ. So they were very close to an even more severe economic crisis.

Mr. YOHO. All right.

Let me ask you, what did we get out of the negotiation? I mean, usually, when you negotiate, there is something that you get. I don't see anything that we got. I mean, we still have four Americans over there that—I don't want to put Americans as hostages and negotiate for them, but I don't see anything that we got to even open up these negotiations. I think we should have carried them on another 5, 6, 7 months, 1 year.

How likely is it—well, if we continue with the negotiations and we extend it, do you see Iran backing off on their ultimate goal of getting a weapon?

General, go ahead.

General HAYDEN. Again, I do not see them backing away from keeping the option open——

Mr. YOHO. Keeping the option open.

General HAYDEN [continuing]. And turning to a weapon.

Mr. YOHO. Mr. Sadjadpour, how about you?

Mr. SADJADPOUR. I agree with the General, in that I have always thought Iran's ambitions are to have the capability, not necessarily to weaponize.

Mr. YOHO. All right. So they want to have the right to do that, is what they are working on.

And so, with the sanctions, they were doing that anyways. All right? They were getting closer to that. Now that we are in negotiation, they are going a little bit faster. They are getting the technology. So what I see is they are going to do it regardless.

What would be the effect if we just pulled out and says, "You know what? You are not playing fair. We don't like the way you are playing. We are just going to put the sanctions back until you are serious about it"? I mean, is that an option that you would recommend?

Mr. SADJADPOUR. I think, Congressman, it is important to contrast the current Iranian Government with the predecessor government of with Mahmoud Ahmadinejad. Two years ago, Ahmadinejad united the international community against Iran. Countries like Russia, China, Europe, which actually have disparate interests vis-à-vis Iran, united around the same policy.

I think this time around it is going to be much more difficult to maintain international unity, especially if the United States issues what I would say are unilateral sanctions against Iran. You may see the P5+1 split up and Iran exploit those divisions, which would be a very negative outcome for us.

Mr. YOHO. I am out of time, and I thank you.

Ms. ROS-LEHTINEN. Thank you, Dr. Yoho.

Mr. Connolly of Virginia.

Mr. CONNOLLY. Thank you so much, Madam Chairman.

In some ways, the previous President—you were referring to the regime blaming the other guy. It took us 4 or 5 years to learn how to pronounce his name, "Ahmadinejad." Maybe we miss that part of him.

I guess I am not sure I am following where this testimony is all going or where my colleagues want us to go.

So would we be better off if we had not had the interim agreement? Should we have just walked away from it and said, no, we don't trust you, we don't like you, we have lots of other issues as well, we think you are headed inevitably to a nuclear capability, and therefore we are not going to pursue the negotiation option? Should we have done that?

General HAYDEN. I will jump in first, Congressman.

The other options are so bad that I, personally, 10 months ago, 11 months ago, that is why I was willing to tolerate negotiations with a state I believed to be a fundamentally unreliable negotiating partner.

Mr. CONNOLLY. Right.

General HAYDEN. I was willing to give this a chance.

Mr. CONNOLLY. So you——

General HAYDEN. But it depends on the character of the agreement.

Mr. CONNOLLY. I agree. But I wanted to get that—I mean, given all other options, we should have pursued this and tried to make it work?

General HAYDEN. Again, given how bad all the other ones were, we needed to exhaust the table before we started to turn to the others.

Mr. CONNOLLY. Mr. Dubowitz?

Mr. DUBOWITZ. Congressman, I agree. I mean, as I said in my testimony, I think that a peaceful resolution of the Iranian nuclear crisis was the right way to go. I think a negotiated agreement is the right way to go.

I think the dispute that is taking place now is between those who are skeptical of Iran and those who may be skeptical but they fundamentally believe that there has been a sufficient change in the domestic environment in Iran and in any interfactional power balance that we should be supporting Rouhani and Zarif against the hardliners and that we have a chance to fundamentally change the Iranian regime's approach to its nuclear weapons program.

I don't believe that there is a fundamental distinction between the so-called moderates and the hardliners. They are all united around a common objective.

I do think that we can do a better job of negotiating with the Iranian regime. I think we—we didn't have to give up four concessions right up front as part of the JPOA and diminish our economic leverage at the same time.

Mr. CONNOLLY. Yeah, and I want to get there, because that is my next question.

But did you want to comment, Mr. Sadjadpour?

Mr. SADJADPOUR. Yeah, Congressman. As Henry Kissinger often says, we have to weigh these major foreign policy decisions not against the ideal alternative but the realistic alternative.

Mr. CONNOLLY. Right.

Mr. SADJADPOUR. I think we would all agree here there wasn't a better alternative than the interim deal.

I would also add that the interim deal has done a few things which have been useful. We got Iran to pull its car over to the side of the road; it is not making forward progress——

Mr. CONNOLLY. Right. And I think that is really important, because—all right, we have now established all three of you agree, given the options, we had to go that route. And I think I am hearing you admit, or say, it is not all bad. I mean, some of my colleagues get carried away maybe a little bit, and you would think that this interim agreement has been an abject failure in all respects. That is not true.

But moving forward, there is the question, Mr. Dubowitz, you were I think getting at, which is efficacy. We want a non-nuclear Iran. If I am hearing General Hayden correctly, your view of history and your view of intelligence is that is an unachievable goal, given what options we have in front of us. The what you euphemistically call the ''kinetic'' option would actually have the opposite effect, you said, which we may want to make sure Prime Minister Netanyahu understands. And we could bomb or take out

Assad's air force. I am not sure, in terms of efficacy, that will deter Iran from pursuing a nuclear option. We can double down on sanctions, which guarantees that Rouhani cannot politically stay at the negotiating table, which effectively will end negotiations and probably seal our fate in terms of what happens next: We either accept the nuclear Iran or we take it out militarily.

I don't see a lot of good options here. And I see Congress doing what it usually does, which is cavil, but not have any helpful solutions in terms of, well, then, what will we do.

Mr. DUBOWITZ. Congressman, I disagree with you, because I don't think Rouhani is going to leave the negotiating table. I think the Iranians are going to stay at the table. I think the fact——

Mr. CONNOLLY. Even if we double down——

Mr. DUBOWITZ. Even if we double down.

Mr. CONNOLLY [continuing]. On sanctions?

Mr. DUBOWITZ. Even if we double down on sanctions.

Mr. CONNOLLY. Huh.

Mr. DUBOWITZ. Because I think that they need to stay at the table. They need to stay at the table because they need to figure out a way to get themselves out from under this international pressure. I agree with Karim. I think that is part of their strategy.

They also need to stay at the table because, for them, diplomacy has actually been very useful—with the Europeans from 2003 to 2005, with us. Diplomacy is the way to move their nuclear program along.

The car is not at the side of the road, by the way. On certain elements of the nuclear program, like 20-percent enriched uranium, we have made some progress, but the Iranians are moving on other aspects of the program. To Congressman Deutch's point, we don't know what they are doing on weaponization. They could be moving their weaponization activities down the fast lane as quickly as possible, and we don't know. Advanced centrifuge R&D. As Olli Heinonen has said, they could have thousands of advanced centrifuges somewhere that we don't know about, and they could be manufacturing them today.

Mr. CONNOLLY. Yeah.

Mr. DUBOWITZ. So it is incorrect, A, to say that the Iranians have no other option but to walk away, because if they walk away and they walk away, they will be faced with a tidal wave of sanctions that will collapse their economy.

And, B, there are inherent flaws in the JPOA that need to be corrected, and a comprehensive agreement needs to be a more effective agreement. And there are very good reports out there and analysis that shows how it can be better. We all agree there should be a negotiated agreement. We just think it should be a fine agreement.

Mr. CONNOLLY. Yeah. I——

Ms. ROS-LEHTINEN. Although your time is over, Mr. Connolly, I know General Hayden would like to respond.

Mr. CONNOLLY. Thank you.

General HAYDEN. Thank you, ma'am.

Congressman, another way of thinking about it perhaps: You think about this as two clocks going. All right? One clock is the clock on the Iranian nuclear program, and the other clock is the potential for change within the Iranian political system. I mean, we don't want to treat Iran like Japan, because Iran is not like Japan, but Iran doesn't have to stay not like Japan forever.

And so maybe one way of thinking about this is what we are really trying to do here is to slow their progress, to slow this clock down, to leave the potential for other developments over here to take place.

And there are a variety of tools to slow that clock down. There are sanctions, there are embargoes, there is covert action, and there are negotiated settlements, duly, carefully arrived at, that make it more difficult for the regime to speed up this clock.

Ms. ROS-LEHTINEN. Thank you very much, Mr. Connolly.

Mr. DeSantis?

Mr. DESANTIS. Thank you, Madam Chair.

Yeah, I just want to associate with what Mr. Dubowitz just said. I think that, you know, more pressure—you know, Iran—it may not ever be possible, I have been skeptical, we could actually come to a negotiated agreement, but, certainly, relieving sanctions, I think, shows them they can get away with more. When you are putting more pressure on them, from their psychology, I think that you at least have a chance.

And that is why, General Hayden, I appreciated your admonition about trying to think like they think. Because I think sometimes some of the folks in the State Department—and I think this is indicative, when the President is writing a letter to the Ayatollah to try to, you know, seek common ground in the fight against ISIS, I don't know that that appreciation is there the way it should be.

Let me ask you this. You had mentioned how Iran looks at something like what happened to Qadhafi and they say, well, gee, why would we not want to have a weapon? I think that is 100 percent correct.

Is it the case—it has been reported, and, kind of, I know we say that around here—that when the U.S. deposed Saddam Hussein in 2003, that Iran halted its program at that time out of fear?

General HAYDEN. The National Intelligence Estimate of 2007, reflecting back on that period, the Iranians did stop one aspect of the program, the weaponization, and not the others. They did. It was coincident with the American move into Iraq, the American presence in Afghanistan, but my analysts, Congressman, were reluctant to draw it as cause and effect.

Mr. DESANTIS. Well, I appreciate that.

In terms of—so we have talked about North Korea, that example. Obviously, that is not a good path for us to follow. It didn't work. And I know it is a tough issue. It seems to me, if you look in the Middle East, the other examples of nascent nuclear states, Iraq in the 1980s, that was neutralized militarily by Israel; Syria, 2007, same thing.

But I noticed there was an article in The Atlantic in which, or Jeffrey Goldberg, Bloomberg—he writes for one of those—where I think he quoted an administration official basically cowing that Netanyahu, you know, he has waited too long, he is not going to be able to do anything. And they thought that was kind of, like, a good thing.

And I just wonder, I mean, if Iran does not fear the potential credible threat of military force, isn't it much less likely that they are going to be willing to make the concessions that we are looking for?

General HAYDEN. It is very important that Iran believe that all options are on the American table. And I am making this distinction, Congressman, because this is not about will, it is about capacity. And the ability of the Israeli Air Force, much smaller than ours, distant from the battlefield and so on, their ability to inflict a punishing strike on this nuclear program is far less than ours. So it is our will, it is our policy that makes the difference and creates leverage in negotiation.

Mr. DESANTIS. And in terms of the kinetic targets, that with Iran's program, we are looking at something that is much more dispersed and difficult compared to Syria and Iraq, correct?

General HAYDEN. The Osiris reactor in Baghdad, al-Kibar in Syria in 2007, a raid. This will have to be a campaign, if it were ever chosen.

Mr. DESANTIS. So the underlying problem with the whole thing with Iran is that, of course, it is led by an Islamic fanatic ideology. And having a new regime there, I think you have millions and millions of people who would rejoice at being liberated from what is essentially a theocratic, authoritarian country.

Now, we know and I think, Mr. Dubowitz, you mentioned 2009 and how there was turmoil. So, today, what are the prospects of more demonstrations? What are the prospects of there being a really credible movement to try to govern Iran in a different way?

Mr. SADJADPOUR. Congressman, the discontent which existed in 2009 hasn't gone away, but, at the moment, I see no prospects for any type of meaningful popular uprising. There is no cohesion to the opposition. And I think, frankly, when Iranians look around at what is happening elsewhere in the region—the carnage in Syria, the carnage in Iraq—I argued that in 1979 the Iranians had a revolution without democracy, and today they aspire for a democracy without a revolution.

I think there is an important point here, because there is a paradox to U.S. Policy toward Iran which I think it behooves us to think creatively about. And that is that I think everyone in this room would agree that the underlying problem we have with Iran is really the nature of this Iranian regime. We are never going to be able to trust its nuclear program is purely peaceful. But the challenge is that the policies that we are pursuing in order to counter Iran's nuclear program, political and economic isolation, I would argue entrenches those very hardline forces in Tehran that we are trying to get rid of.

And I think it is important for U.S. policy to think about being aligned with the aspirations of the Iranian people for greater political and economic integration rather than being aligned against those aspirations of the Iranian people.

Mr. DESANTIS. And I am out of time, but if you could for the record maybe submit some examples of what we can do policy-wise. Because I think that that would solve a lot of problems in the region.

Ms. ROS-LEHTINEN. Thank you so much, Mr. DeSantis.

Mr. Schneider of Illinois.

Mr. SCHNEIDER. Thank you, Madam Chairwoman.

Again, to the witnesses, thank you for sharing your insight here, but thank you, more importantly, for the work you have done and continue to do. What happens in Congress can't happen without the work that you do. But I also want to emphasize that I don't think the United States and the international community can effectively stop Iran without the work Congress does, so, again, to implore the chair and the ranking member to continue on that.

Mr. Sadjadpour, I want pick up on something you said in your opening remarks, and that was the prospect—there is so much we need to focus on, but I want to stay focused on Monday, on the 24th—the prospect of a partial agreement on Monday. The principle was and the need for a comprehensive agreement 1 year ago was that there would be nothing agreed to until everything was agreed to.

So I guess I will throw this to the whole panel. What happens if there is a partial agreement? What does that do? What is the consequence of that? And what actions must Congress take, in that case?

Mr. SADJADPOUR. Congressman, I think that when both sides and, frankly, when all sides—China, Russia, our European allies, United States, and Iran—when they contemplate the alternatives to failed negotiation—potential return to status quo ante, potential escalation, potential conflict—I think everyone appreciates the fact that, even if it is not possible to meet in the same place to comprehensively resolve this issue, it behooves all sides to try to continue to work forward and at least extend the negotiations.

What happens afterwards? It is my sense that if you can lock in Iran's current compromises, they are not making forward progress, and continue to deter forward progress, keep them in place, that is not a bad option for the United States. It is what I call "managed irresolution." I think if you have a scenario whereby they remain 1 year away from having a nuclear weapon, we have averted a conflict in the region. That is not a perfect outcome, but, compared to the alternative, it is not a bad outcome.

Mr. SCHNEIDER. Okay.

Mr. Dubowitz?

Mr. DUBOWITZ. So, Congressman Schneider, I would say this. First of all, Iran is about 2½ months away from breakout as a result of the Joint Plan of Action, which means the length of time it takes to weaponize a sufficient amount of uranium for a nuclear weapon. We actually don't know, as General Hayden has said and others have said, what is happening on the weaponization side. So we actually don't know how far Iran is from having a nuclear weapon. We know they are 2 months away from having weaponized uranium for a bomb. So the status quo is fragile, to say the least.

The second thing is, regardless of what happens on Monday—I will get back to my original testimony—we have to maintain sufficient leverage through these negotiations. And that is economic leverage, it is political leverage, it is a credible threat of military force. My fear has been, since signing the JPOA, that our economic leverage is diminishing.

And now you, as Congress, are in the position where the administration has said to you, we are going to bypass you with respect to sanctions relief. And so, as I detail in my testimony, there are 12 recommendations about how you can build a sanctions relief firewall, how you can ensure that what you are putting in place will maintain some of the toughest sanctions. It will give a phased and smart program of phased sanctions relief and that you can maintain that economic leverage.

Because whether it is a comprehensive deal, a partial deal, an extension of the JPOA, at the end of the day the Iranian regime is salami-slicing us, and they are stretching out these negotiations. They are diminishing our economic leverage. They are giving up concessions on the nuclear side that are reversible.

That is the key. Nuclear concessions they give up are reversible. Sanctions relief that we give up is irreversible.

Mr. SCHNEIDER. I agree.

And I just want to give General Hayden the last word with two other small questions to that. Because I do think, if there is to be sanctions relief, Congress has to have its voice heard.

But, to your point, you talked about clocks, and you also talked about the term or duration of an agreement. How far back do you think the clock has to be set, in an agreement moving Iran from decision to breakout capability, to be effective? And how long do you think that agreement has to stay in place to be viable and to give us something that we can count on?

General HAYDEN. I would begin my discussions at at least a year. Okay? And I would begin my discussions with indefinite. And I don't mean——

Mr. SCHNEIDER. I agree.

General HAYDEN [continuing]. To be flippant. I am quite serious.

Mr. SCHNEIDER. No. I use the term ''generations.'' But it can't leave the people in power today in power when this agreement ends.

All right. With that, my time has expired. Again, thank you for what you do. And thank you to the chair and the ranking member.

Mr. DESANTIS [presiding]. The gentleman's time has expired.

The Chair thanks the witnesses for their time and their testimony. We learned a lot, and we very much appreciate you taking the time to come.

And, with that, this hearing is adjourned.

[Whereupon, at 2:45 p.m., the subcommittee was adjourned.]

APPENDIX

MATERIAL SUBMITTED FOR THE RECORD

SUBCOMMITTEE HEARING NOTICE
COMMITTEE ON FOREIGN AFFAIRS
U.S. HOUSE OF REPRESENTATIVES
WASHINGTON, DC 20515-6128

Subcommittee on the Middle East and North Africa
Ileana Ros-Lehtinen (R-FL), Chairman

November 13, 2014

TO: MEMBERS OF THE COMMITTEE ON FOREIGN AFFAIRS

You are respectfully requested to attend an OPEN hearing of the Committee on Foreign Affairs, to be held by the Subcommittee on the Middle East and North Africa in Room 2172 of the Rayburn House Office Building (and available live on the Committee website at www.foreignaffairs.house.gov):

DATE: Thursday, November 20, 2014

TIME: 1:00 p.m.

SUBJECT: Examining What a Nuclear Iran Deal Means for Global Security

WITNESSES: General Michael Hayden, USAF, Retired
                    Principal
                    The Chertoff Group
                    (*Former Director of the Central Intelligence Agency*)

                    Mr. Mark Dubowitz
                    Executive Director
                    Foundation for Defense of Democracies

                    Mr. Karim Sadjadpour
                    Senior Associate
                    Middle East Program
                    Carnegie Endowment for International Peace

By Direction of the Chairman

The Committee on Foreign Affairs seeks to make its facilities accessible to persons with disabilities. If you are in need of special accommodations, please call 202/225-5021 at least four business days in advance of the event, whenever practicable. Questions with regard to special accommodations in general (including availability of Committee materials in alternative formats and assistive listening devices) may be directed to the Committee.

COMMITTEE ON FOREIGN AFFAIRS

MINUTES OF SUBCOMMITTEE ON _____ *Middle East and North Africa* _____ HEARING

Day___ *Thursday* ___Date___ *20 November 2014* ___Room_____ *2172* _____

Starting Time ___ *2:00 PM* ___Ending Time ___ *2:45 PM* ___

Recesses | *0* | (____ to ____) (____ to ____) (____ to ____) (____ to ____) (____ to ____) (____ to ____)

Presiding Member(s)

Chairman Ros-Lehtinen; Rep. DeSantis

Check all of the following that apply:

Open Session ☑   Electronically Recorded (taped) ☑
Executive (closed) Session ☐   Stenographic Record ☑
Televised ☑

TITLE OF HEARING:

Examining What a Nuclear Iran Deal Means For Global Security

SUBCOMMITTEE MEMBERS PRESENT:

Chairman Ros-Lehtinen, Raking Member Deutch, Reps. Chabot, Cicilline, Connolly, Cotton, DeSantis, Frankel, Higgins, Kennedy, Kinzinger, Schneider, Vargas, Wilson, Yoho.

NON-SUBCOMMITTEE MEMBERS PRESENT: *(Mark with an * if they are not members of full committee.)*

None

HEARING WITNESSES: Same as meeting notice attached? Yes ☑ No ☐
(If "no", please list below and include title, agency, department, or organization.)

STATEMENTS FOR THE RECORD: *(List any statements submitted for the record.)*

SFR - Rep. Connolly

TIME SCHEDULED TO RECONVENE _____
or
TIME ADJOURNED ___ *5:00 PM* ___

Subcommittee Staff Director

Statement for the Record
Submitted by Mr. Connolly of Virginia

After a year of intense and extended negotiations, we are now on the eve of the November 24 deadline to achieve a comprehensive agreement that will prevent Iran from developing a nuclear weapon while significantly constraining and establishing close monitoring of its domestic nuclear program. Throughout the talks under the Joint Plan of Action, I have remained cautiously optimistic that the P5+1 and Tehran could reach such an agreement. Though I was encouraged by progress that extended the discussions last summer, we must now deliver on the promise of this historic opportunity.

The P5+1 negotiations represent the first meaningful engagement the U.S. has had with Iran in decades. However, let me be clear, it is Iran's own actions that have sent it down a dark path of world isolation and economic stagnation. Tehran's illicit nuclear program has drawn international condemnation, and the Islamic Republic has been subject to broad and effective sanctions as a result of its provocative actions.

The deplorable human rights situation in Iran has been an additional cause for ostracism. I was pleased to join the Chairman and Ranking Member in support of H. Res. 754, condemning the Government of Iran for its gross human rights violations. It is a testament to our foreign affairs apparatus that we can engage Iran and urge simultaneous progress on several fronts and in a variety of venues.

Iran's past transgressions have led to the enduring and profound lack of trust of Tehran by the U.S. and the international community, and we remain in a formative period of engagement with Iran. For this reason, verification, transparency, and compliance must be the foundation of a high-quality final nuclear agreement.

On that front, we have at least some hope. The International Atomic Energy Agency (IAEA) recently reported that Iran has complied with all JPOA obligations. No new centrifuges have been installed by Iran, construction has been halted on the heavy water-moderated reactor at Arak, 5% uranium-235 stockpiles remain at pre-JPOA levels, and 20% uranium-235 stockpiles have been eliminated. To continue this progress, we will need inspectors on the ground conducting daily and surprise inspections.

As I said before, I am cautiously optimistic negotiators can reach a high-quality final agreement with Tehran. I urge the P5+1 to continue pursuing negotiations so long as those efforts halt Iran's nuclear program in the interim and prevent Iran from developing a nuclear weapon. It is my hope that Congress can play a constructive role in this process, and I look forward to our discussion today.

www.ingramcontent.com/pod-product-compliance
Lightning Source LLC
Chambersburg PA
CBHW080523290526
45790CB00006B/2285